THERE MUST BE HONOR

Also by Ken Williams:

China White
Shattered Dreams, A Story of the Streets

THERE MUST BE HONOR

On a journey through life and death and
war, a man calls out for justice and hope

KEN WILLIAMS

iUniverse, Inc.
New York   Bloomington

There Must Be Honor

On a journey through life and death and war, a man calls out for justice and hope

iUniverse books may be ordered through booksellers or by contacting:

iUniverse
1663 Liberty Drive
Bloomington, IN 47403
www.iuniverse.com
1-800-Authors (1-800-288-4677)

Because of the dynamic nature of the Internet, any Web addresses or links contained in this book may have changed since publication and may no longer be valid. The views expressed in this work are solely those of the author and do not necessarily reflect the views of the publisher, and the publisher hereby disclaims any responsibility for them.

ISBN: 978-1-4502-6409-9 (sc)
ISBN: 978-1-4502-6410-5 (ebook)
ISBN: 978-1-4502-6411-2 (dj)

Printed in the United States of America

iUniverse rev. date: 10/29/2010

For my wife, Donna, who has made all things possible.

PREFACE

This book is a collection of articles published locally, along with writings unpublished that reflect the twin tragedies that I have experienced on my journey through this life: the Vietnam War and homelessness; interspersed throughout the book is my autobiography. Names in quotations have been changed, and, in a few instances, case characteristics and personal stories have been blended. For clarification, in the Table of Contents, in italics are the titles of prior written articles. These articles, in the main body, are also in italics.

No amount of whitewashing or pretending otherwise will change the shame of homelessness in our society or erase the general pain of war, which our nation seems to have embraced, or the particular horror that was Vietnam. The truth is the truth.

In many ways the Vietnam War and our treatment of the homeless are similar. The tactical police sweeps of our streets mirror the search-and-destroy missions in Vietnam. Both attempted to move the "problem people" away from populated areas. But after the sweeps or missions were completed, those who lived in the areas in question simply reoccupied the territories. Those who lived in the jungles of Vietnam or on the streets of America needed only to survive to defeat such strategies. Survival trumps weapons of mass destruction and gentrification. However, the survivor's victories are hollow; those in power blame the victims and use prejudice and dehumanization to cover the defeat of their plans. The homeless continue to die by the score while we avert our eyes from the slow-motion train wreck.

ACKNOWLEDGMENTS

Chuck Blitz, Alison Allan, Elijah Allan-Blitz, Gary and Ellen Bialis, Dave Peri, Roger Himovitz, Rosemary Varesio, Nancy Alexander, Bob Klauson, Sarah McCune, Nick Welsh, Jan Fadden, Jan Ingram, Dr. Lynne Jahnke, Jeff Cotter, Lady Leslie Ridley-Tree, Ken, Jo, and Clifford Saxon, Joe and Emily Allen, Sue Adams, John Jamieson, Cath Webb, Margaret Matson, Morris Bear Squire, Cindi Sundberg, Dr. Andy Gersoff, Kaye Theimer, Peter Marin, Merryl Brown, John Buttny, Sandra Copley, Laurette Stern, Debbie McQuaide, Teena Grant, and Mike Nichols.

Special thanks to Jim Buckley; Paul Wellman; Steve Lopez; Marianne Partridge and the *Santa Barbara Independent*; William Macfadyne and noozhawk.com.

CONTENTS

INTRODUCTION

I was scared and lightheaded. Weakness draped her arms around me as if I were a long-lost lover, her cool embrace chilling me to the core. Hoping against hope, I tried to will my suddenly weak knees not to give out. The air trapped painfully inside my lungs became heavy. No matter how much I tried, it was all but impossible to force oxygen past my stone diaphragm. Forget even trying to swallow. My mouth was as parched as the deserts east of LA. The buzzing sound, like a swarm of bees trapped in my ears, set my mind spinning, making rational thought all but impossible. My world had become pure emotion. As in other situations where decision making became crippling, "damned if you do and damned if you don't," I forced myself to simply put one foot in front of the other. Anything was better than the gut-wrenching pain. Or so I thought.

Slowly I approached Joshua, fear impeding each step. I do not consider myself a coward, but it was too much. I swore that it would be the last time I came to one of these things, a vow that I was to break only a few times over the next ten years. That was saying a lot, because the crack and AIDS epidemics that were to cut through the homeless community with cruel efficiency were still to come.

Thank God Joshua's parents weren't there. I wasn't sure how I would react to their presence. It wasn't that my heart didn't go out to them, especially to his mom. But issues remained between us: too many encounters on the streets, with Joshua in tow. Too many conflicting moral issues were outstanding, and now was not the time to deal with them. And Vietnam cast its long, heavy shadow even there—always Vietnam, a living, fiery presence that I could never outrun.

I found myself standing alone next to the baby's coffin, his pale, impossibly tiny body cocooned within. Shock and dread clawed at me, ripping my insides to shreds. How incredibly small the coffin was. Briefly a slow-frame movie flashed though my mind: I saw myself pick up the coffin, tuck it under my arm, and storm off, taking Joshua away from the tragic play, this madness. This was America. That particular horror is reserved for poor Third World countries. Babies don't die on our streets—not in the richest country, the richest state, one of the richest cities in history. But then reality, my reality, Joshua's reality, returned.

I looked down. How peaceful he looked—how small he looked. Someone had put a dollar bill in his tiny hand. Was that supposed to be a statement of some kind? Wasn't his death on American streets enough?

Thank God his eyes were closed. I wondered if that was because no one wanted to see his accusing stare from the beyond. No one wanted to take responsibility. Maybe I should, as a social worker for the homeless. But the agency I worked for, the Department of Social Services, didn't view me as such, not back then, not for another ten years. Maybe they do now, but that's not what my job description said back then.

Technically, my job was to help General Relief (welfare) recipients fight through all the loopholes and roadblocks that the government set up to discourage disabled poor people from receiving Social Security. All that other stuff—billions of office hours and uncountable visits to the homeless shelters, low-income hotels, and soup kitchens sprinkled around Santa Barbara like afterthoughts—wasn't what I was supposed to do. Finding the disabled and discouraged homeless in those shelters and on the streets and trying to help them steer a course that would lead to a life of normalcy just wasn't on the agency's radar. The unofficial plan of many in the public and private sectors was to move them on to another community—to any place but Santa Barbara.

Then there were the miles of streets I covered every week, searching out the homeless; discovering who was still alive and who was in an advanced state of crisis: those who, due to medical neglect, untreated psychosis, or crippling despair had given up hope and greeted death with welcoming arms. The more mundane, run-of-the-mill crises—lack of food, shelter, or appropriate clothing—that would kill most housed citizens were relegated to mere background noise.

As I still do now, I searched out those who lived in the bottle or found solace in a needle or crack pipe, plus the legions of the mentally ill who ran from the terrors of their diseased minds and the judging stares of some of the more fortunate citizens of Santa Barbara. I sought them out not only to offer services but, even more importantly, friendship. When all else was impossible, when housing was priced out of existence and death lurked in the shadows, friendship was still possible. Who could deny even the most strung-out drug addict, washed-up alcoholic, or spiraled-out mentally ill person the one saving grace that we all need? It cost nothing—if you ignored the chunks of your soul that were chipped away by the pain that you shared in the process.

Did I feel privileged that I had managed over the thirty-five years that I had worked for the county to convince (outmaneuver) the system into allowing me to do what my conscience dictated me to do? Or had I merely survived: the last man standing, while others moved on to more prestigious and better-paying jobs, leaving me with my passion for service to those without hope?

Or should I feel angry that the system—the hodgepodge of city, county, state, and federal government entities that the poor must relay on for survival—has failed so miserably in dealing with this modern-day plague?

The first is of small comfort, since it involves only me and my life. On the other hand, my anger reflects how thousands in Santa Barbara and millions across the land have been relegated onto the streets, with trash cans as their restaurants and cardboard boxes their condos; their lives appear inconsequential to our society's mad dash to ever-greater profits and comfortable lifestyles. Society has little room and even less tolerance for those who falter in the race, the casualties of the barbaric economic times we live in: the poor in general and those broken by drug addictions and alcoholism, cursed by the terror of mental illness, or the idealists whose only claim to fame is survival in the midst of this man-made disaster.

Book One

Vietnam

CHAPTER ONE

I enlisted in the Marine Corps in the spring of 1968 while still in high school. It was a time when the country was being torn apart by the war in Vietnam. My greatest fear then was that the war would end before I had a chance to fight in it. I had been conditioned that serving in the military during wartime was the most honorable thing a man could do, that fighting and dying for the noble cause, in this case anti-communism, was of the highest moral imperative. When I was six, I used to have my parents take me to the post office so I could collect recruiting pamphlets, which of course helped shape a naive mindset in an impressionable young mind. I saw every war film that was ever shown on television at least a dozen times. They were all filled with danger, but of course the hero always lived, and the concept of "collateral damage," the butchering of innocent men, women, and children that all wars inflict, was not to be seen. No, for me, war was honor, an adventure—a passage into manhood that I could hardly wait to take part in.

The first jolt to this fairy tale came in 1968, when a Marine that my younger sister had begun a written correspondence with stopped by to visit upon his return from Vietnam. I was impressed with his dress greens but even more so with the war ribbons that he wore over his heart. I saw myself in a handful of months standing there before me. But then reality rudely intruded. Taking me into my bedroom, away from prying ears, he asked me why I wanted to join the Marines. Why did I want to fight in Vietnam? The catch in his voice, the cloud that floated before his eyes, his sight lost to another reality, which in time I would come to recognize as the thousand-yard-stare, jumbled my reply. He wasn't buying whatever conditioned reply I gave him.

In the face of all that seriousness in a suddenly claustrophobic room, my reply became even more choked and inarticulate, a fumbled response against his real-world experience. He told me not to go, that none of it was what I thought, or what he had thought before he had gone there. Of course, being eighteen, I thought I knew better. I had all the worldly experience and wisdom of youth that I needed. After all, I had been taught by the best propaganda that celluloid could provide. He left soon, his emotional scars challenging my naivety, leaving me with my delusions shaken but still intact. I should have listened.

A few months later on a hot August day, an old bus transported us to the Marine Corps Recruit Depot in San Diego. Surely the Marquis de Sade had designed the sticky seats we sat in. The hot, heavy air buzzed with charged electricity that was generated and amplified by each of us and onto each of us—green recruits facing the great unknown. Our childhood dreams were about to come crashing headlong into reality, a slow-motion car crash impossible to avoid. The bus suddenly came to a jarring stop just down the street from the base entrance. Looking at one another, our jumpy stares questioned, *Why?* The bus driver, a man who I assumed was a World War II veteran, rose from his seat and faced us. Reaching behind him, he pulled a lever, and the doors popped opened with a loud *whoosh*. "This is your last chance." We tried to hide our shock from one another, with little luck. Warm, fuzzy speeches about patriotism, maybe bawdy banter were expected, but not this in-your-face warning. Only later, looking back, did I realize the hell this man must have gone through: week in, week out delivering up youth to the vengeful god of war. How many boys had taken their last bus ride with him? How many came back horizontal in metal caskets? How many faces haunted his dreams at night?

With a heavy heart that seemed to age his face right before our eyes, he looked us over, searching for one boy who would take his advice. When none of us did, his shoulders slumped. He turned, and the door slammed shut. Within seconds, the bus lumbered past the guard post, and we officially belonged to the Corps—The Green Machine. We stumbled out of the bus and into purgatory. The shouts and yells from the DI that followed were a blur. The next three months that I spent there seemed more like a decade.

Not particularly athletic at that time, my body was pushed and prodded in more ways than I thought possible. What kept me going was my need to graduate, complete my basic training at Camp Pendleton, and get myself into the war before it ended. That the war would end soon was an overriding concern, knowing as I did that nobody could stand up to our military superiority and moral righteousness. How they had managed to survive the pounding of the last three years was beyond my naive comprehension. It dawned on me years later that I had spent my entire childhood with that war as a background, not just three years, and that there had never been an end to it in sight. Not in my wildest nightmares did I imagine that the war would drag on in one form or another for seven more years. Even today I can still remember that some of my earliest childhood recollections were of radio news about American deaths in a faraway land called Vietnam. Why we were unable to beat a small insurgency all those years before was the question that our political leaders should have been asking. It was obviously beyond the immature thinking of a boy.

In boot camp, cracks began to form in my mind-set —early warning signs that things were not as they had been presented by the government and media at the time. The first one was the misogyny I encountered—the fear and hatred of women and the view that they were less than men. The most vile, prejudicial language that could be imagined was directed not only at us, but also at women by the feared drill instructors. If you screwed up in any way, fell behind in calisthenics or forced marches at all, you were called every word for female anatomy that was found as graffiti on bathroom stalls. The United States Marine Corps, the defenders of Western civilization, held half of the American population in such low regard; even a kid like me knew something wasn't right.

And then there was the racism, the need to dehumanize based solely on race so we could butcher, kill, and wipe the *enemy* from the face of the earth. It was said that the brutalization was necessary so we wouldn't hesitate to kill when the time came. But at what cost? What do you do when the need for survival destroys what you set out to defend—what you hold most dear within yourself? When you discover that, in the final analysis, the only thing that separates you from the so-called enemy is that you're the last man standing.

What wars really come down to is that the best killers claim the moral high ground. It's the natural Darwinian process that drags civilization backward every time it engages in war. Those who hesitate to kill because of their moral training are more likely to die than those who enjoy it. Of course, most of us fell in the middle, just trying to survive one more day.

"Kill VC!" we shouted a thousand times a day, not only when we practiced bayonet training or shooting but also at seemingly innocent times, such as getting up from a mess hall table after a meal, or after an academic lesson in killing or the proud history of the Corps.

Gook. Dink. Slop Head. Rice Eater. Fish Head. These vile words were screamed at us and by us with unimaginable hatred until the Vietnamese were no longer human beings. Any hateful and hurtful name that we could come up with to dehumanize the enemy, to sanitize the blood-letting, to hide the fact that we were being trained to ignore the first commandment, *Thou shall not kill*, was encouraged. Suddenly, for the first and last time in our lives, it was not only okay to kill but, in fact, against the rules *not* to kill.

Sadly, not till a stopover in Okinawa on my way to war, when I heard a fellow Marine use one of the racial slurs against a "shoe shine boy," an elderly gentleman the age of our grandfathers, did I realize that the terms I had grown comfortable with were in fact racist. I had assumed that they referred only to the communist enemy. My embarrassment, the pain that froze my heart when the words were uttered in front of this man, acknowledged the true intent of their racist nature. The language wasn't just against the enemy; it was against a race of people different from us in skin tone but still people nonetheless. These words—more like accusations—were used to turn people into the "other," simply because of skin color. It was a harsh lesson that racism cannot be contained. By its very nature, racism demands that we look at people who are different from us as lesser than us. It forces us to devalue that difference and, in the process, poisons our hearts while destroying our moral foundations.

It's not easy to turn American kids into killers. It should have been a hell of a lot harder to convince America's parents to hand over their children to a government that lied and cheated us into war. It is a lesson still unlearned, for we still hand over our children to politicians who run foreign policy based on outright lies, for which they are rewarded with another four years by a democratic society.

CHAPTER TWO

During War, Hatred Becomes the Enemy

Noozhawk.com, 8-7-09
The sweet smell of diesel fuel hung heavily in the air. I could barely discern the muted sound of rock music. In our imaginations we might taste ice-cold beer, though deep-down we knew it would be warm. Chilly beer was reserved for officers only, back at base. The illusion of ice-cold beer was a good match for our multifaceted dislikes—we hated everybody who wasn't us. Only Marine grunts—the ground-pounders, the riflemen, the machine gun and light mortar crews of our company—escaped this hatred. We hated the flyboys in the Phantom jets, Broncos, and Puff gunships, unless they were saving our skin by killing the enemy wholesale. But even they got only a brief reprieve. We hated the guys in tanks and armored personnel carriers (APCs) and choppers, because they never had to hump the tortuous mountains or the humid, killing lowlands. We hated Ricky Recon and the woolheads of the Green Berets, who, after spending a few days in the jungles and mountains, were able to return to somewhat secure rear bases where hot showers, real food, and bunks with blankets awaited them—luxuries that bordered on the fairy tale level for us.

Years later I realized that we hated everything because, mostly, we hated ourselves. We hated the hopeless situation that we found ourselves in. We hated the fact that idealism, or sometimes the raw circumstances of life, had entangled us in a deadly web of lies and deceit, while the rest of the country went on with their lives as if we didn't count. We hated the fact that we had volunteered for duty and country, while the rich kids got deferments or went into the National Guard. We intensely hated the hatred that we discovered within ourselves, the things we did out of fear, and the brutality that the human race is not only capable of, but at times seems to wallow in. Finally, we hated the fact that we were stuck ten thousand miles from our families, with perhaps no way home besides a cold and indifferent coffin.

I sat on guard duty that night so many years ago at Con Thien, a fire support base just below the DMZ—the thin strip of land that separated North from South Vietnam. Fifteen APCs and tanks had drawn into a circle just outside the razor wire that surrounded the base, which offered us a faint illusion of security. The mass armor of the vehicles contributed a threatening, beastly essence; the arrogant aura about them threatened death to anyone stupid enough to cross their path. They were like the Viking gods of destruction, daring the mortals of earth to play the game of death with them. With cannons defiantly tilted upward and a sea of machine guns leveled low, with mounted spotlights and heavy steel draped about them, they seemed invincible to a lonely Marine on guard duty at two in the morning. Yes, hatred and envy came easy   at least till the next evening when I again pulled guard duty.

During the day, we heard that the armored caravan had ventured north, looking to deliver destruction and mayhem upon the enemy— the men of the 324B North Vietnamese Division. I envied them a little less now. At dusk when I relieved the Marine before me of guard duty, I looked out at the wire, looking for Death. Nothing. Inside the wire to the left, where the road left Con Thien, three dark green APCs were pulled up tight next to one another. The Marine I was relieving followed my line of sight, saw the question in my eyes, and said, "That's what's left of them." I'm sure I tried to hide my shock and then the shame of my emotions from the night before. Pain rang out loud in my heart. The armored beasts looked forlornly beaten down—sad. They had found the enemy and only partially was it the NVA. The real enemy was pride and the harshness of violence.

Death was the real victor. I wondered what the young Marines inside the APCs and tanks felt when rocket-propelled grenades (RPGs) rained down on them like hail; when the APCs turned into deadly infernos of flames as their thin skins succumbed to the storm of explosives that torched the onboard fuel. We used to call the badly burnt and horribly mutilated Marines who had been caught inside those fiery death traps "crispy critters."

Fear also played me. If those primordial beasts could so easily be reduced in twenty-four hours to the pitiful remains before me, what chance did I have—did any of us have? And a new thought found fertile ground. What of the people of this land? What chance did they have as the ancient war gods played their twisted games of fate, with all of us as pawns? And could I not even have the pure emotion of hatred to hold onto? My contempt for the men of armor and air and ship, and eventually of the enemy themselves, turned bitter in my throat. I had judged others harshly for the stupidest of reasons. And I had traveled ten thousand miles to kill those who believed differently than me, also for the flimsiest of reasons.

As Conrad, author of The Heart of Darkness, so insightfully wrote, the enemy was to be found within our own hearts. If the price of hatred was to be found anywhere, it was here.

Postscript: Shame

"The pending backlog of unprocessed Veterans Administration disability claims now stands at over 400,000, up from 253,000 six years ago," according to the New York Times.

"The VA's claims backlog, which includes all benefits claims and all appeals at the Veterans Benefits Administration and the Board of Veterans Appeals at VA, was 803,000 on Jan. 5, 2009. The backlog hit 915,000 on May 4, 2009, a staggering 14 percent increase in four months."

February 1969. Da Nang, the Republic of Vietnam. Of course it wasn't a republic. It was a military dictatorship. I remember the day clearly, like it was yesterday's dream—yesterday's nightmare. It was the day I landed in the middle of a war aboard a 727. Sadness leaked from the stewardesses eyes, bleeding from their souls. How many of the boys they were taking to war would never return? Stepping from the plane, humid air smacked me like a profound physical force. I had never known that air could be so heavy, feel so oppressive.

We waited for half a day in a stifling hot room, while we, the replacements, were assigned to different units. Waiting with us were a few combat vets returning from R&R or hospital leave. Ominously, they kept telling us to avoid the 9th Marines at all costs. When we timidly asked why, they would only tell us the unit's nickname before they turned and quickly walked away, like they were cursed for merely saying the words: The Walking Dead. Somehow that unit's nickname was supposed to be explanation enough, all by itself. When we asked around as to where that unit was stationed, we were told that they were currently in the A Shau Valley. Those words were also spoken in a whisper, once again leaving me with a feeling of dread, similar to what I had felt as a kid watching a horror film. It began to dawn on me that I had ventured into something that was way beyond my ability to comprehend or understand, for sure beyond the experiences of my life. I also came to appreciate that this new reality could easily kill me. And if I should survive, it would change me in ways I couldn't even begin to guess.

This strange new world that I had stumbled into, where hidden meanings and allusions to death were suddenly part of the landscape, was reinforced when my orders were given me: Charlie Company, First Battalion, Ninth Marine Regiment, Third Marine Division—the feared Walking Dead. This new *Alice in Wonderland* perspective on my life was shoved in my face on the bus ride to a forward base, where I was to catch a chopper to join my new unit. Over the windows was barbed wire. When we asked about its purpose, we were informed that it was to prevent the citizens of Da Nang from lobbing a grenade in the bus.

Death becomes personal in war. At times he was the other side. At other times he was the new guy with the squad or the old, salty Gunny. He could appear in the jungle, in the night, on a dusty trail, in the deadly bite of a pesky mosquito, or even in a different war, another time. Enemy or friend? The only thing for sure was his presence, the reality of his mission.

Snapshots of War Remain Vivid

Noozhawk.com, 11-10-09

The tank reared up like a wounded elephant and was thrown skyward, perpendicular to the ground that had hidden the anti-tank mine. The tank I was riding on was to the right of it and slightly behind, giving me a front row seat. A cloud of rising dirt and black smoke quickly engulfed the enraged tank. Out of that dust storm, the body of a Marine shot high in the air and backward, in free flight. I was close enough to get a good look at his face. I expected anger, fright, pain; instead, I saw a bizarre calm acceptance.

I exchanged harried glances with the other grunts riding on top of the hot metal tank before we jumped down, switching off the safeties on our M-16s, preparing for the ambush that we knew awaited us. We burrowed into the high, sunburned elephant grass, trying to see into the foreboding tree line immediately in front of us. All was deadly silent; no incoming or return fire, only the roaring of tank engines as they circled their wounded comrade. An image of circling Triceratops, horns pointing outwards to ward off an attack, came to me. Looking back, I could not see the Marine who had been blown into the air.

The tank-led assault had started innocently enough. Anytime we grunts could ride rather than walk on our unending sweeps of the plains surrounding Con Thien was a blessing. It was just too hot and the terrain too unforgiving to have it any other way. Of course we didn't like the fact that this mission was intended to draw enemy artillery fire from across the DMZ. The purpose was to locate their 155s and 175s long-range artillery inside North Vietnam so when the current bombing halt collapsed, the Air Force would again have something to bomb. It made us all feel like bait dangling on the end of a line. But that's what being a grunt was all about. Your life was part of an equation, a mere calculation in an absurd game, with death as the scorekeeper. And until the roar of the explosion cracked the morning, it had been an easy ride.

Lying prone, with my nose inches from the hard-baked soil, I saw others begin to stand and look quizzically at the ground. I slowly stood, keeping an apprehensive eye on the tree line. There at my feet, orange plastic tape encircled a rather large rectangle. Similar marking tapes were found all over the field. The word was quickly shouted from one Marine to another: "Mine field!" We stood frozen. This was an anti-tank mine field, judging from the force of the blast that could blow a several-thousand-pound tank into the air like a kid's toy. And it had been marked off. What the hell was going on?

It was an old mine field left over from the days when the French thought they could tame the Vietnamese. Our engineers had come before us to mark it off, in anticipation of our supposedly fast-moving tank sweep. Had the NVA observed them? Had they moved some of the anti-tank mines around to blow an unsuspecting tank? Or had an officer simply misread a map and sent us into harm's way? The only sure thing was the comical sight of a heavily armed company of Marines delicately, cautiously stepping and getting back on the tanks, praying like hell. We vowed vengeance should the tank driver stupidly ignore the tread tracks of the tank in front of us and strike out on his own.

But before getting back onboard, we refilled our canteens with water from the bomb craters scattered around us. I didn't relate the chemical taste and oily film on top of the water to the event of the evening before. We had sat on our bunker overlooking the wire at Con Thien, shirts off, flak vests on, watching the sun setting behind the towering mountains off to the west. The flight of three cargo planes, flying low in a shallow V-formation, caught our attention. The pristine white mist they released gently flowed to the ground, catching the rays of the setting sun like fog settling. It was beautiful and graceful in a peaceful way.

Agent Orange wasn't really orange. That was the color of the bands they put on the barrels to identity its deadly cargo. Nobody ever bothered to warn us about its deadly effects. Nobody told us not to drink water from the sprayed land. Nobody told us anything. As the grunt motto of the war went. "It didn't mean nothin'." Nothing meant nothin' there, but of course it did.

Weeks later, we were deadly tired. We had wasted the day in the boiling sun, hunting the NVA in a God-forsaken valley deep in I Corp. Sweat and grime coated our bodies, and thirst tore at our parched throats. Why anyone would want this piece of real estate was beyond our imaginations. The boys at the Pentagon, the NVA—whoever wanted it could have it. The only thing we knew was that we grunts didn't.

We had been entertained with random artillery explosions and had had the privilege of watching our mortars fly overhead, stall, and plunge to earth. And of course, the brilliant display of napalm never failed to impress. The only confirmed body count (partial) was a foot blown off at the ankle. I tried not to think about it, but how could I not? Had he lived? Had he become a cripple for the rest of his life? After all, what good was a farmer without a foot? Had he either crawled away or been dragged away by his comrades to simply bleed to death? He was the enemy, yet more. He was my comrade in all this suffering.

The mission was complete; waiting for the tanks, our ride back to camp, we let our guards down and began congregating, and then the bullets began to fly. Persistent cracks from AK-47s broke the air. I dived head first into a bomb crater. Suddenly everything went silent. I crawled to the top of the crater and looked over. Just as I did, a lone NVA soldier opened up on me—only on me. The bullets dug into the ground below me. I felt the impact of the bullets as they walked up the side of the crater. The last one flew by so close that I felt the air being compressed by it. Half an inch, maybe a quarter of an inch was all that separated me from a deadly head wound. I felt hurt, emotionally. This was personal. He hadn't sprayed his rifle fire. It wasn't an impersonal bomb, mortar, or RPG. He had taken careful aim, waited for me to peek over the edge, and then tried his best to kill me. I asked myself what I had done to him to deserve this. Why was he mad at me? But the impersonal nature of war was the whole point. It was an abstraction against an abstraction. Him—me. An instrument of death against an instrument of death. Except, of course, the abstraction was me—my life. I took it very personally, probably the same way my comrade, who had lost his foot and now lay bleeding to death, felt—a future suddenly gone bleak. In the end, it was all very personal.

The Present

   Veterans from numerous wars, wounded in mind, body, and spirit, continue to call the streets home. Studies show post-traumatic stress disorder (PTSD) levels approaching 25 percent for Iraqi and Afghanistan veterans. According to an article in the Los Angeles Times, the average suicide rate of eighteen per day among veterans waiting for their disability claims to be adjudicated is escalating. Before yet more are sent into harm's way, we owe ... "Some gave all. All gave some."

CHAPTER THREE

War was not what I expected. Some talked about putting a bullet in their leg to get out of that hellhole. I remember the day that the talk became reality for a good friend of mine. The look in his eyes when they carried him away on that poncho has stayed with me all these years. It was not something I had prepared myself for. How could any nineteen-year-old kid do so such a thing? How was I supposed to understand his doing so? What reference should I look to for an explanation? Nor did I know how I felt when the sergeants came around and collected all side arms. No one would be stupid enough to shoot themselves with an M-16. That powerful weapon would blow off a leg.

And how do I regulate the memory of a man who I knew was courageous throwing down a can of M-60 ammo when enemy machine gun fire opened up? I remember starting to bend down to pick up the ammo can, but the bullets impacting into the tree next to me—mere inches from my head—led me to another choice. Or my hesitation about offering a fellow wounded Marine a helping hand, not because of death exploding all around us but simply because I was exhausted, almost too tired to care if either of us lived. And what would have become of me if I hadn't helped him and then saw that he didn't make it onto our chopper? Or if he hadn't made the next chopper—the last one to leave that hell? Of course, that would have become guilt piled on top of guilt. All that guilt wouldn't, and didn't, crystallize till my stay on the hospital ship, a part of the journey months in the future. No, war was not what I had been brought up to expect.

War as Evil

unpublished

 God, please, no nightmares—no more dreams of war. That was a futile prayer if there ever was one. I had just finished the summer issue of Vietnam Magazine. It ran an article on Anthony Poshepny, a CIA field agent who served in Laos during the Vietnam War, the character that Colonel Kurtz in the movie Apocalypse Now was based on. With a nod and a wink, the article told of this colorful man and the many legends about him. The tone of the story was boastful and comradely: he was one of us, a combat veteran, larger than life, a man who knew how to fight—and fight well. To me, he was simply a symbol of everything that was wrong with war. He was a man bent by the evil of war, proof that war is evil, a sickness forever lurking in the darkest recesses of the human soul.

 The magazine story told of the practice of beheading the enemy and putting those heads on pikes and dropping them onto the houses of suspected enemies; in one case, a head was dropped from a low-flying plane and bounced into a home. This was done by an American in our name, supposedly for us. How the author could portray this without moral revulsion is beyond me—or maybe not. Such is the corrupting power of war; idealism rapidly turns to Satan's tools and inhumane practices that we would normally condemn, which we all too quickly find justification for. How is it we recoil in horror (as we should) when terrorists use beheading as a tactic in Iraq but give grudging admiration to similar American tactics, which our government turned a blind eye to?

 An example of the dehumanizing ways of war is the attempt to justify torture by simply redefining torture. Is this much different than when dictators claim that the end justifies the means? How about the notion that the means are the ends? How about the idea that America stands for something decent? That as a people we are somehow special, a nation that others once looked up to—even our enemies? After all, it was not the Russians that the civilians of Nazi Germany fled to in the closing days of World War II. It was us.

This particular article reminded me that we once praised General Pao (and some still do), a Laotian warlord, who fought a C.I.A. funded war against the Lao and Vietnamese communists. He not only employed terror as a tactic (all in the name of fighting terror— sound familiar?), but was also hip-deep in the drug trade. He was apparently a man who turned a dime off of dope, ignoring all the pain that that dope was causing American soldiers, Marines, and sailors trying to numb the horrors of war.

This colorful CIA agent also was in the practice of paying for the collection of human ears, a gruesome atrocity that soon spilled over to Vietnam. The story told of how he ran across one child whose ears had been cut off by his own father so the poor family could collect promised bounty money. How many other children and women's ears were likewise collected? How much did this sick man's practice contribute to the degradation of life that so characterized Vietnam?

And today, evil under the cover of war once again walks the land. The sadistic practices at Abu Ghraib were the direct result of putting Americans in harm's way, of pretending war is Hollywood, of leaders spouting the justifications that torturers have used throughout history. The brutal killings in Haditha, if true, are proof that evil has once again been set loose upon the land. Part of the calculus of war must include the question, How many vets will come home to be forever tormented, forever maimed, by what they did, by what they saw?

For me the glory, the honor, the esprit de corps of combat will be forever reduced to a horror show called a hospital ship: to a small boy horribly disfigured by napalm burns; a young mother turned into a freak before her baby's eyes by a blast burn or napalm; to a black man, gut shot, in excruciating pain; to a Marine on our ward, withering in his death throes.

A car in front of me this morning carried a yellow ribbon sticker: SUPPORT OUR TROOPS. Want to support our troops? Bring them home. Not six months from now, not a year from now—yesterday. Stop the next war before it starts, before those sick power groupies in Washington threaten to invest our children as if they were oil to be fed into an SUV.

When do we grow up, take responsibility, and stop these stupid but excruciatingly sadistic games? Enough is more than enough. No more war, no more ears as trophies, no more severed heads as a tactic. No more glorification. No more. Evil is war. War is evil.

No more lies—they stop now; they stop with us.

CHAPTER FOUR

The A Shau was where it all began to turn. Up till then, the only exposure that I had had to violence was the occasional fistfight at school. To suddenly find myself in a place where violence was a way of life *and* death was a shattering experience. Till then, life had followed cause and effect along crystal-clear scientific lines. To experience the unscientific, inexplicable look of death in another's eyes and a lifeless arm dangling from under a poncho set in motion a chain of events that would end in the total transformation of who I was, what I was to become. The A Shau was one end of a set of bookends; the other was my stay on the hospital ship, *USS Repose*. The next story captures the emotional hangover between the two experiences that transformed my worldview, which was built upon the clouds.

Haunted by the Past, Not Quite Ready to Vanquish It

Noozkawk.com, 4-20-09

    The dates that fracture time annually roll around like clockwork— so maddeningly predictable and yet so unavoidable. My mood turns less joyful at first, then quiet, finally becoming grim. Sudden sounds become hauntingly terrifying. I look around to see if anyone has seen me jump—self-conscious, ashamed. The compressed events fall into sequential order. First came the terrifying helicopter ride into hell—the highlands of northern South Vietnam, where the 9th Marines and the soldiers of the NVA 324B Division were locked in mortal combat. The playing field was the miles-long A Shau Valley, a primordial, fog-shrouded, triple-canopied mountain range that looked and felt like I imagine prehistoric Earth must had been.

Then came the fear and the confusion of combat, the ear-popping explosions, and the gut-wrenching acknowledgment of mortality, when I felt the physical presence of death as an entity for the first time.

Time becomes hallucinatory on these anniversaries, bending back onto itself; the future becomes the past, which in turn invades the present. It all becomes confusing and terrifyingly real. I look at the clock, check the calendar, and become transported back to that place and time where both become one, suspended in the world that exists between then and now: It's morning; there's no food. I look up and see stars, cursing and blessing the absence of fog. The choppers can land; we can get out of hell, yet only then can the final battle commence.

I hear the guttural sound of that long-ago early morning; a forlorn M16 cut loose, chasing away demons in the dark. I know what to expect next: the green tracers of answering enemy rifle fire. Machine guns join the musical score next. I remember the short round that was already on its way, so-called "friendly" artillery fire that would explode just feet in front of the bomb crater where I took refuge. It tossed me to the bottom of the crater in a surreal yet deadly cloud of splintered wood and razor sharp steel shrapnel. A blinding white light and a death-defying roar pressed in all around me.

At this time of year on the drive to work, the days begin to run on. The ambush lands in the middle of the road, out of sequence— that's already happened. Today is the day when the enemy will crawl through a sea of napalm and a storm of steel left by bombs and artillery shells. I once again suck the taste of hot and heavy air into my lungs. Hopeless despair compresses my heart as the jet fighter bombing runs and artillery strikes creep ever nearer, delineating just how close the enemy has managed to get—how close my unit is to being overrun.

Enemy mortars intensify the fear as they search out the helicopters. If the enemy cripples the landing zone, they eliminate escape. But then the weariness of it all catches up to me. I'm too hot, too hungry, just plain too exhausted to care anymore. Anything, maybe even death, is better than this. When the enemy machine gun rounds strike the tree inches away, an unconscious part of my body kicks in, propelling me forward without willful thought. The slow-motion sprint to the waiting chopper is like running through sand. The door gunner's look of fear and his frantic gestures to hurry up and get on board momentarily stun me. Then he cuts loose, delivering a river of steely death that tells you something evil and decidedly fatal is right behind you. The building racket of bombs going off, mortars impacting the earth, and automatic weapon fire shredding the air all around me bleeds into the present. Then I remember; I look down and see the grenade—that grenade.

Time elapses—time passes. The calendar turns; I survived another year, another anniversary. My dark smile informs death, "Not this time, not this year." I try to gently push the memories back, to confine them to the anniversary dates, or to the times when something in the present jars my defenses. What I need to do is force time back into a linear rather than a circular form, an impossible task that even Einstein was unable to do. It's called survival.

In a few months, I went from a green rookie, a willing participant in an insane war, to a weary combat veteran hating the war, what it did to us, and what it had forced us to become. We walked more miles than I thought possible through those primordial mountain jungles, in searing heat and monsoon downpours that surely hadn't changed since the dinosaurs ruled the land. My ideals had been shattered. The war had made a mockery of my faith in my country. The only good thing was that I still didn't have the luxury of trying to figure out what I would do once I got out of there—if I got out of there—my rotation date was still too far into the future. Death was my more immediate concern. He had all our attention.

Apache Snow was a typical search-and-destroy mission, light in "official" combat casualties but heavy in emergency medivacs. I remember one time when we had set up a defensive perimeter at the foot of a mountain, with an artillery base at the top. Just as the sun was dying, loud explosions rocked the base above, shattering our false sense of well being for the evening. The pyrotechnic display went off for hours, and then the black night crushed in all around us.

The black sky was filled with the sound of choppers taking out the wounded and dead.

Some said an NVA rocket had hit stacked ammo. Others said an incoming helicopter had been hit. And still others reported that the re-supply chopper had crashed, touching off the explosions when its cargo cooked off. Which is the whole point of war. Did it matter to the Marines who were wasted that night if their deaths came at the hands of hostile action or something as mundane as an accident? The only thing for sure was that if it weren't for the cruel war, they wouldn't have been on that cursed mountaintop deep in the A Shau. They wouldn't have died. They would have lived to marry, father children. Some would have perhaps gone on to add to the cultural or intellectual heritage of our country. We'll never know how many Einsteins died there or doctors that may have discovered the answer to the riddles of cancer, stroke, or AIDS.

Maybe I'm wrong. Maybe the calculations were made somewhere in the back corridors of the Pentagon and Washington. In the hushed, out of the way offices of power, the equation was made that as long as the casualties were black, brown, and working-class white, it all factored out. We were the acceptable collateral damage, along with the Vietnamese, of course. Draft deferments and National Guard allotments would take care of the sons of the wealthy and powerful, of those who mattered, in their worldview.

The Foreverness of War

Noozhawk.com, 3-26-10

To this day, the sound of choppers can bring a Vietnam combat veteran's world to a halt. Sometimes it brings back the hash bark of machine guns and the roar of rockets spraying the jungle and forest— the winged messengers of death. Other times it's the remembered smell of rot, the heavy odor of napalm, or the stench of death from some god-forsaken battlefield. For some it's the bone-jarring, death-defying dive of a chopper skirting enemy fire as it deposits them into combat. For others it is the rapid take-off of a life-saving chopper, away from the Grim Reaper's playing fields. It can still seem very vivid after all these years. For me, especially in the quiet of night, the memory is of the forlorn sound of dust-offs—medical evacuation choppers coming in to take the dead, dying, and wounded away from all the butchery. Two separate incidences roar back into my consciousness, as dust-offs, like bellowing warhorses hidden by the blackness of the night and the fog of war, alight out of thin air:

The lines are stretched thin. A single Marine is assigned to each shallow fighting hole, which means an all-night, 100 percent alert. No sleep—again. Tanks and armored personal carriers pull into a tight circle below us. We are one ridgeline over—a football field away, as the crow flies. Then tremendous explosions from the circle of tanks and APCs rip the night apart, shredding our fragile sense of safety. Flames shoot high into the air. Exploding anti-tank claymore mines torch metal, barbecue flesh, and broadcast trembling shock waves that crash into us. Night vision becomes another casualty.

Fear hangs heavily in the air—sharp and repugnant, reinforced by our aloneness. Tank cannons, machine gun fire, M16s, and AK-47s play a madman's symphony. Flares, in no particular hurry to join the carnage below, float lazily down, casting ghostly images, highlighting death's obscene dance. Again, the darkness of the night turns into a macabre light show, as burning metal and still louder explosions envelop us. Marine artillery fire adds thunderous volume to the mix, soon to be followed by Spooky, a slow circling plane, an airborne gun platform with automatic Gattling guns sending death at thousands of rounds per minute. The sound of AK-47s creeps closer as NVA soldiers situated on the ridgeline between us and the circle of death open up, keeping us pinned down.

The sound builds to a crescendo, then ... silence. Soon, the soft thump of chopper blades can barely be discerned. They grow louder and louder, becoming hypnotic—luring us into a rhythmic trance. A strobe light comes alive, signaling an improvised, supposedly safe landing zone. It is a rock concert light show in the middle of hell. Choppers buzz in, unseen; they land for seconds and then shoot into the void with their sacred cargo. Silence follows, as if the dead are talking to one another, to be followed by more helicopter blades piercing the sky, their thumping sound mere feet above us. All night long. All night, then—now. The dead, the dying, and the rest of us. Mind games. What if? Why?

Months later, we again find ourselves in the high mountain jungles along the Laotian border. We have spent weeks humping the impenetrable jungle forest with little sleep, sparse food, playing deadly games of cat and mouse with the NVA. We are run down with exhaustion and heat. Morale is low. Malaria is in our blood, but we don't assign our night sweats, nor the day chills, nor the semi-hallucinations caused by the fevers, to it—yet. We are dug in just below an artillery fire support base. A thick jungle forest separates us. We hear a lone supply chopper coming in. We hear it land. Then explosions erupt from hell. Next day we hear tales: accidental cook-off of artillery shells? A lone and lucky hit from harassing NVA artillery? Or perhaps the chopper simply crashed? Take your choice of excuses that Death rides in on. One massive explosion is followed by another one, and then they begin to run together. Stored artillery shells are definitely cooking off now. Death paces maniacally throughout the firebase, turning it into a meat grinder.

Thankfully, the pyrotechnics finally end. Deadly shrapnel stops slicing through the night air. As if from Norse mythology, salvation for the survivors or transportation to Valhalla comes on the back of unseen choppers slipping in unseen through the night. I expect to hear Wagner music. Again, all night long, hour after hour, the dust-offs come in and take off, pounding that distinct sound into your brain. The beating blades invade my troubled dreams, then—now. What was the final toll of that night? How much blood was sacrificed to the war gods? Do they ever become satiated? Did this have to happen? Whose sons, husbands, and friends died that night? That sound, the thump of dust-off choppers, becomes engrained, a part of me, as I am part of Vietnam. It's the foreverness of war. No forgetting the memory of Vietnam—no forgiving: the ultimate gift of war that combat veterans have bitterly learned over and over again for the last 10,000 years.

Updates

ABC news reports that at least 8 percent of men and women in the armed forces are being medicated for psychological problems, including antidepressants, such as Prozac, Zoloft, and Paxil. "We are sending soldiers into the field, into combat missions, who are suicidal," said former Air Force psychologist Jason Prinster. An earlier report found increased suicide rates among younger veterans. We cannot replay Vietnam—it must not happen again. It's time to bring our soldiers and Marines home and help them and their families heal.

County Mental Health is proposing that they drop treatment to the uninsured. Not only is this immoral, but we will see even more mentally ill people wandering our streets without treatment, severely impacting them, their families, our community, and our spiritual beliefs. And, as hard as it is to believe, the Community Kitchen is under heat for feeding hungry people during the worst recession in eighty years. Are the poor really supposed to go hungry in times such as this?

It's strange, but after all these years, I can still remember the exact moment when I turned against the war intellectually. The deeper moral opposition would come for my time on board a hospital ship, the *USS Repose*.

I was sitting with rifle in hand, my brain boiling under a hot metal helmet, staring out at the jungle across a cleared field of fire at C-2, a Marine fire support base deep in Leatherneck Square. It was a part of northern I Corp that the Marines thought they owned. Of course, so did the North Vietnamese Army. For the bragging rights of ownership of the coastal lowlands to the mountain jungles further inland that bordered Laos, men, by the thousands and then tens of thousands, from both sides died. With thirty-year hindsight, I've come to see that we were one and the same, the so-called enemy and ourselves: soldiers sent by politicos to kill each other and die in the process. We were, are, a fraternity of arms—men and women who endured the same leeches, malaria-bearing mosquitoes, hot lead, and sacrifice. We were a metaphorical couple, caught up in the dance of death, with neither one of us paying much attention to the conductor. And in the end we were united forever by our sacrifices to the gods of war. We are the brotherhood of shared misery, lost youth, wasted lives.

That particular day was hot and clammy. Sweat poured down from my forehead into my eyes, filling them with stinging salt. The acknowledgment of the waste of it all bolted into my brain, like lightning. There before me was the all-too-real, impossible-to-deny truth: With all the material we were literally blowing up and wasting, we could easily have built a better world a thousand times over. Why did we organize such huge expenditures of resources to kill one another, instead of using them to address the social issues in the world and back home that were tearing our country apart in the 60s? It all seemed so simple, sitting there. It was a revelation, a conversion of sorts. All we needed was the willpower to redirect all the wasted energy.

That startling insight kept my idealism intact. My calmly reasoned opposition left the center of who I was unchanged. It would take a heavier blow to shatter forever the boy sent over to participate in the noble experiment that I had been led to believe in.

So I turned against the war intellectually but not emotionally, not morally. Before I was forced to cross that bridge, my soul, my being, needed further preparation.

CHAPTER FIVE

My body and mind were prepped. My soul still needed working on. The mindset of a naïve nineteen-year-old was being transformed, but if I thought my journey was finished, I was sadly mistaken. So far, the war had drawn pain from my fellow Marines and me. But something important was missing from the equation, something that was to shatter forever my concept of war as a noble enterprise.

The first symptoms of malaria hit when I was swimming across a river to string a rope across so others could cross the fast-moving, deep water. Incredible weakness came in waves, like a crushing tide, robbing me of so much strength that for a moment I feared going under. I figured it was simply exhaustion from walking too many miles in too-high heat. After all, we had been humping these mountains without rest for almost a month. But the weakness grew exponentially, till hours later, the patrol that I was with left me and another Marine at the side of the road, covered with flak jackets; we were too weak to continue, and they were too tired to give a damn.

To this day, I still cannot understand how I allowed myself to be left like that or why they would do that. It was another unexplained mystery of war to add to all the others. We could have easily been killed or captured. But that was nothing new; we all made stupid decisions at the end of an operation, after weeks of racing through those mountains in the boiling sun stole our ability to reason, our sanity, and, for some, the will and purpose to live.

A few days after the incident on the road, the unit pulled back to STUD, a forward Marine base situated between the DMZ and Laos. While standing in formation, vertigo forced my hand. Within minutes, an evacuation helicopter was called in. On board the chopper, a corpsman slapped a needle into my arm, and fever-busting fluids were pumped into me.

I spent the night at a hospital in Da Nang. Waking in the middle of the night, I found my arm painfully swollen. I called the corpsman over. Sheepishly, he informed me that the needle had slipped out of the vein and fluids were being injected into the muscle of my arm. He reinserted the needle, and I gratefully passed out. The next morning the decision was made to evacuate me to a hospital ship.

Ice Princess

Santa Barbara Independent, 5-24-07

Her smile was brief and guarded, her eyes hidden, her soul deep. Most turned their gaze towards her, and those that didn't were too far into their own pain, their own fear, to care. Her white, sharply pressed uniform contrasted with the loose-fitting blue hospital gowns that we wore. And to think that days before we wore sun-bleached tattered uniforms caked with sweat and mud, adding another layer to the surreal that flushed onto this nightmare.

There was another reason why some diverted their stares. She was labeled the Ice Princess by many of the boys in men's bodies in the hospital ward. They observed and felt how she refused to return their boyish flirtations. Her demeanor was chiseled, stern, and serious. Putting aside our juvenile attitudes and fantasies about seeing an American woman after months of only seeing Vietnamese women was next to impossible for most of us. And why should that not be? After all, we were boys sent to war to do the manly thing and kill or be killed. I was nineteen—couldn't vote, couldn't drink. While my friends from high school back in "the world" (as we called home) went off to college to enter adulthood slowly and grow gently into the mysteries of sex and relationships, I entered the age-old hell of war, where men were twisted and then broken by the brutality of war, all for the lies of politicians who wouldn't send their own sons to die for a lost cause. But they would send us, the selected few, to a Dante's inferno, where a woman and a child horribly disfigured by the glory of napalm were the bit players, the walk-ons, for sick men safely hidden behind their wealth, by their student deferments or connections with the National Guard.

As is often the case with men, we label women cold, ice, unreachable, when we can't fathom their pain, when they don't respond to our obvious sexual appeal. For some reason, this nurse took an interest in me. It may have been because of her determined effort to break the one-hundred-and-five-degree temperature that threatened to fry my brain, if not kill me. I remember her stripping my bed of the mattress cover when I had crawled under it, shivering from the fans that she had aimed at me. I remember her taking blood samples from me four times a day for two weeks, trying to find the telltale signs of Falciparum malaria that was rampaging through my body. I remember her caring when all I wanted to do was hide from the diseases ripping me apart, from the hell of war that I had gladly volunteered for and was now trapped within.

During my recovery from malaria, typhus, and dysentery, we became friends. The other Marines and soldiers were jealous. Why did we talk in hushed tones? Why was she the way she was? Gently, quietly, she told me how she hated the war, how she hated that ship of horror and why she was stuck on board the USS Repose. Her purpose, her secret, was one of great courage, inspired by love. She had a younger brother in the army, and as long as she was in a war zone, he was safe. It was against policy to have more than one member of a family at war at one time. There were only weeks to go before his enlistment was up.

Here was a woman who did what she hated, hating what she was forced to see day in and night out, in order to protect her brother, a woman who was forced to withdraw and hide behind a sheet of ice to protect her vulnerable soul from the brutality of war. The war machine was like a meat grinder, using patriotic slogans and outright lies to seduce unknowing youth to be used as cannon fodder. It chewed up the bodies of Vietnamese women and children like a ravenous wild boar.

During uncountable hours that passed as slow-moving torture, she saw the broken bodies and bent minds coming and going, and she withdrew so she wouldn't snap. How does one process the hushed rumors putting bounties on the heads of officers, spoken in the shadows by fellow Marines and soldiers? Or the stories told by the survivors of Hamburger Hill of the needless slaughter of soldiers sent repeatedly up its deadly slope, only to abandon it once the ravenous gods of war had been fed? Or those of a country laid to waste and a proud culture deformed till the sex and drug trades became the go-to economy?

The last time I saw her, she held a white letter crumbled in her hand. Her brother had passed the magic mark and could no longer be posted to Vietnam. She was skipping down the hallway of the ship, her nurse's shoes softly tapping off the walls of the sick bays that held broken bodies to her left and right. Her brother was safe—she had insured that with her own personal sacrifice. The ice was melted, and relief sparkled in her eyes. Lonely, terrifying nightmares still lay before her, unknown but guessed at, but her brother would live. Now she could go home—victorious, with honor.

My intellectual turn against the war had involved no deep soul pain. But the overwhelming emotional pain from that ship killed the boy sent off to war. In his place a man, partially crippled by his guilt for participating in such an evil endeavor as war, was born. The horror of busted bodies and twisted minds that I had been given but a glimpse of in the field became an overwhelming reality aboard that ship. And to add weight to all that pain was the suffering of the civilians—the children and women, the innocents caught up in the ultimate macho fantasy of war.

Veteran's Day 2000: Memories

Santa Barbara Independent, 11-00

You see, I know I'm dead. Well, at least pretty sure. Sometimes not knowing is as bad as knowing. But if I'm dead, then what am I doing here? Maybe this is purgatory, that place we go to when God is undecided about whether we are going to heaven or hell. I think that's the idea behind purgatory. I wish now that I had paid more attention in Sunday school when I was a child. But back then, the purpose of purgatory was the farthest thing from my mind. Important things like the new girl in class and if the surf was up at Huntington Beach were of far more interest. But now, there is no more pertinent question.

The dreaded time draws near. I know this when I look down at my hands and see them bathed in sweat. I try to wipe them dry on my baby blue hospital jimmies, but to no avail. I squint when my eyes tear from the salty sweat that rolls down into them. At least that's what I tell myself. But I know better. I look around me, and everyone I see is also having difficulty with tears—ah, I mean salty sweat.

It's an unnerving sight, this collection of rugged nineteen- and twenty-year-old warriors with so much sorrow in their eyes. Still other eyes are framed by pain, guilt, and the madness of terror. Why are they spending time in purgatory? But then the thought comes to mind that maybe I'm not dead. After all, does a spirit feel the sting of tears or the dampness of sweat?

Maybe I'm just mad, or better still, maybe I'm in a dream. That could be. I've been sleeping a lot, nineteen, twenty hours a day, the last two weeks. That is, till the nightmares began to chase me out of sleep and into this waking hell—ah, I mean purgatory.

I look around for a clock, but the mess hall—a military restaurant, for those not in the know—has no clock. In fact, neither does it have doors or windows, another reality-bending quirk. Nothing unusual, really, as this is a ship, a hospital ship. To be precise, it is the USS Repose on duty off the shores of the Republic of Vietnam. The time is the bloody summer of 1969, a period when evil walked that foreign land.

I prepare myself the best that I can, for the apparition is always on time. Like clockwork, he struggles in, dragging his left leg. That's not accurate; he drags the entire left side of his body. My stomach goes into convulsions as it did the first time I saw him. I look around and see others grimace with similar reactions. Still others turn away, refusing to look at him. Forks stall in mid-air, and what little conversation there is dies with a hallowed echo. A strange reaction from this tough and bitterly learned group of men.

Our reaction is so much stranger because the apparition is at most five years old. His eyes are large, round, and almond color. He too diverts his eyes so that he looks at no one. He wears the same baby blues that we do. They do little to hide the hideous scars of the napalm burns. Half of his burnt face has melted, flowing like so much water, only to become one, a frozen river of raw flesh uniting face to shoulder. That accounts for his awkward gait. It also accounts for the weird bend to his left arm that forces him to carry it with his right one. The human body, made in God's image, has been rearranged by the scientists at Dow Chemical.

Bile rises in my throat when the boy walks past me. My eyes focus in on the angry wound, dead center on his left shoulder, where the liquid fire devoured flesh all the way to bone. The boy appears to be trying to lift his head, held at an artificial bend, but he can't. I am sure that the fragile mind that endured such horror can no longer be straightened either.

I swallow the bile and get up to leave. I am too weak of flesh and mind to know what to do or how to do it. I know that I'd like to take him in my arms and comfort him, but how? I'd also like to tell him I'm sorry, sorry for what happened to him, to me, to all of us. But the evil that has visited us has created too much pain, mistrust, and hatred to allow me to do that.

Sadly, I realize that evil has won an important round. It feeds off the pain of the little boy and others, so many others. It also feeds off the hatred that is endemic to war, in particular, this war. And it leaves a calling card. Those of us touched by evil, forced to come face to face with it, are compelled to look for the evil in everyone and for the violence we know that is always lurking around the next corner.

I guess that I know now that I knew then that I wasn't really dead, though the hallucinatory fog that I existed in on that ship of horrors may have left that impression at the time. As for being mad, perhaps I was then and perhaps still am now. The boy visits me frequently in my dreams, and more times than I care to count, when I look at my sons I see his face, his essence, in them. At those times I curse the men, the lies, the pride, and the stupidity that brought us that war. And I curse that part of myself that fell victim to them. But I honor both veterans and civilians who stood tall in the face of evil. To paraphrase Robert F. Kennedy's eulogy: those who saw the suffering then and tried to stop it, who see the suffering today and try to ease it.

There is nothing noble or glorious about war. We best honor those who served by observing that ancient truth. And if we hand down that truth to each generation, then we take away the victory that evil claimed during those times. And perhaps the suffering of that little boy and all children wounded and maimed by war would be eased by such an effort. A lesson that can only be learned at such a cost is truly a bitter and fragile one. But it's one that must be learned.

I came away from that ship not sure where to put the blame: On myself? There was no way not to. With my country? Only on the war? Or was it all wars? I came to the conclusion that with the first shot of war, we all lose. That whatever the reasons for war, once it is let out of the bottle, evil is born, and the causes fall by the wayside. Then evil not only feeds off the acts of war but powers its most hideous aspects.

When mutilated children walk among us, the finger of blame points to us all—to all adults who not only do not step forward to protect them but offer excuses about the unavoidable necessity of their suffering instead. The self-serving justification of "collateral damage" only deepens our collective guilt. Children's bodies, children's innocence, can never be taken without the tacit consent of those adults who do nothing to prevent it. After all, isn't it the very essence of nature, of the natural world, that one generation is there to protect and raise the next, not to slaughter them in the name of the ideology of the month? And when we fail to do protect them, then we fail at all else.

I may have questioned where to put my guilt, but guilt's pain needed no such contemplation. It found a home deep within me and managed to manifest itself in a thousand questions. How could I have volunteered to participate in this evil endeavor? How could I speak of the horrors of war when I lived and others didn't? Did I have any right to any feelings about the war because others had had it rougher than me? Did the guilt's pain mandate that I speak out or shut up and hide my role in the insanity of war? Over the years, these questions would battle with one another for supremacy. An example of this was my hidden status as a war vet. Even though I became very active in the anti-war movement in college, hardly anyone knew of my service in Vietnam. When I was a social worker years later, an outreach nurse whom I knew well was surprised when she found out that I was a war veteran.

But the time came when I was forced "out." The country's drifting amnesia about what had happened in Vietnam—the pain, the cost to others—forced me to speak out the one way I found I could, by writing. And years after that, I found the moral justification to do so. During the run up to the Iraq War I ran across a book by a Vietnam vet who had become a Buddhist monk. It's message moved me deeply when he said it was our duty as war vets to speak out against the horrors of war.

Maybe the Quakers say it best: To witness evil. Loosely translated, it means that we must not turn our eyes from evil but see it in its entirety, tell others about it, and by that witness hold accountable those who perpetuate it. It is a belief that evil finds a nurturing environment in the dark, that our hope as a species is to cast a light into those dark corners where evil flourishes and to display the practice of evil before all, for all to see.

I left the hospital ship a changed man. In addition to the carnage I witnessed, two books that I found on board were to have a profound impact on my life. One was: *I Never Promised You A Rose Garden.* The other one, by an author whose political philosophy I would come to reject but whose characters I hotly embraced, told of one man's struggle against the faceless evil of the time and of another's disillusionment with the cause he once embraced. The book talked of the individual's struggle against complacency in the presence of faceless evil.

Ayn Rand's novel spoke to me across the political divide that separated us. It also taught me that no one has a monopoly on truth. Even those seen as the opposition can claim at least a part of the truth, as long as we are humble enough to keep an open heart and not let preconceived ideas blind us to the truth.

What also tore at my soul was the realization that when the news camera lights went off and the media wandered away and citizens moved on with their daily lives, those affected by the war remained in its shadow and would continue to do so till the day they died. Often I asked myself how we were supposed to tell the burnt boy, the mutilated mother, or the gut-shot Marine that they were the ones to pay the horrible price for what was soon to become an outdated idea? How could we look them in the eyes and tell them that the containment of communism, or, for that matter, ethnic cleansing for a greater Serbia or war to rid Iraq of Saddam Hussein, justified their suffering? How do we tell them the truth: that their suffering was all a mistake, a slight miscalculation of history? That it was a mistake that would cost between two million and three million lives? When do the lies stop? And when has the outcome of war ever had anything to do with the original reasons for war?

I had volunteered for war. Not only had I enlisted willingly, enthusiastically, into the Marines, but I had volunteered for duty in Vietnam, or at least I had tried to. I can still see the grin on the various sergeants' faces when I made repeated requests to do so. To a man, they told me not to worry. They told me that the casualty rates were so high that every marine in my various training units was going over there—guaranteed. That should have been a warning, but I was too young and too idealistic to hear the wolf at the door, couched in those cold words.

CHAPTER SIX

Coming home was a shock. While mine had been shredded, life had gone on normally for most. Cars were bought; schooling had begun for my friends and the first hesitant steps toward careers and building families taken. I felt bitter that the country still functioned as before—nothing had changed. I wanted to get off the bus and shout, "What the hell is the matter with you people?" How could lives go on when evil walked the earth? When violence to an unimaginable degree was a way of life half a world away? If it was hard on me, it was equally hard on my family. Walking into the apartment complex where my parents lived, WELCOME HOME signs draped from the balcony, was a bitter experience. I wanted none of it. I wanted the war to go away, but I also wanted it to be everywhere—up front, in everyone's face. I wanted it to consume everyone like it consumed me, day in and day out. And I wanted those responsible for it to be punished.

I had always been a history buff. Not only had I seen every war movie ever made but also documentaries by the ton. I had watched *Victory at Sea* many times, caught up in the soaring musical score and the heroic warrior message. But now I avoided war movies, except those about Vietnam.

I remembering trying to be the person that I was before by watching a documentary on the Pacific campaigns of World War II. A scene of a Japanese Zero being shot down broke me. All I could see or feel was a young man dying, flames searing his conscious with incomprehensible pain. His intense aloneness, knowing he would never again see his loved ones, would never love again, or, for that matter, ever see another human being, overwhelmed me. I had never felt so all alone in my life as at that moment. To me he was simply a lone human being dying an agonizing death, stripped of any honor

37

to the homeland or to the warped ideology of Imperial Japan. He was only a fellow human being dying in overwhelming isolation.

But films and books on Vietnam were my addiction. The war was an open wound that constantly needed picking at, a sore; an infection that I had no resistance to. In the most profound way, I looked to books and movies on the war to confirm, and to some extent to validate, what I had experienced. Deep inside, I questioned my sanity, my take on reality. Had I really fought there? Had there even really been a war?

America was too good at compartmentalizing the war. Society was too good at keeping it tucked away, especially as it wound down in the years following the collapse of the Southern forces. That they needed to ostracize the veterans of that war to do so was the unacknowledged tradeoff, something that nobody wanted to either admit or speak about but that most silently embraced. In many ways that is the guilt that today's America carries; the veterans of that war were asked to pay twice, once in actual combat, once by a society that made them represent a bad hangover, a memory best repressed by shunning vets.

I never talked to my family about the war, and they never asked. They were probably too busy trying to figure out where the son and brother that they had sent away to war had gone. They were too busy trying to figure out how to dodge all the anger that boiled within me.

I went to college, got a degree in psychology, and became a social worker for the poor and homeless in Santa Barbara. But the war continued to haunt me. The war was a part of me that not only refused to die but also festered, inflicting pain on America and her vets years later.

To Be Brushed by Evil

Santa Barbara Independent, 5-24-01

I guess when one has brushed up against evil, the experience increases one's imagination. At least that is what I attribute the memories to that often keep me awake at night and too often color my waking hours. But one doesn't need much of an imagination for the pictures that flashed though my mind when I read the accounts of former Nebraska Senator Robert Kerrey's exploits in Vietnam. After all, we have the scene from the Oklahoma bombing of the fireman carrying that poor little girl in his arms as he steps gingerly from the ruins. That picture is still too fresh, too heartbreaking, and too present in our thoughts and memories. Only now we need imagine that the man carrying the body is Vietnamese, as is the little girl he holds in horror. We can see her dangling arms wave casually back and forth and her long black hair fall in waves toward the darkened soil of the Mekong. Her chocolate-colored eyes glaze over with the horror that she was forced to witness at such a young age. The stoic face of the man—friend, relative, concerned villager—crumbling under the hammer blows that must have strained his heart and cursed his soul as he pulled her body from the pile of dead and laid it gently aside.

It was hard to follow the reportage of the killings that long-ago night. It's even harder to accept Kerrey's versions of the events. People don't just conveniently bunch together so they can be quickly killed. For those who have not had the privilege of having someone trying to shoot you to death, your first instinct is to scatter and try to become one with the earth.

But even more chilling are the accounts of the first hooch. A woman, an old man, and three little children were butchered by knife. Did Kerrey help carry out these cold, bloody murders as alleged, or did he just stand by while others under his command did so? Did he not hear the cries for mercy, of pain? What about the cries of injustice as children were knifed to death—up close and personal? If true, those killings were not carried out by scared nineteen-year-old-youths with minimum training but by twenty-five-year-old men who were supposedly highly trained professionals.

And what are we to make of the political elite in Washington and the cultural elite in Hollywood and New York scrambling to justify Kerrey's actions? How dare they justify his action by context! They are going to have to explain very carefully and very slowly how the murder of innocent children is justified, context be damned. Maybe it has more to do with Kerrey being one of their own than it does about those dead children. And don't they realize the insult they do to the veterans who fought there? With their morally bankrupt defense and Kerrey's own actions, they give credence to the hateful charges of "baby killers" that were hurled at some returning veterans.

It is imperative that veterans do not allow the political establishment to compromise our own personal moral standards again. The men I fought with, the men who cycled through that hell, would be the first to offer their own lives to protect children. They were not and are not killers of the defenseless and innocent. And it is not only imperative but also natural that we be the ones to protest most loudly against attempts at justifying those murders. It is fitting that it is we who hear and are moved by the anguished voices of the children as they cry out for justice from their graves.

This may be our last chance to reclaim the honor that was stolen from us. If we do nothing now, if we don't push for a trial, then we go to our graves with history judging that honor, or lack thereof. And most important, we must remember the true victims here, regardless of how they were killed: the twenty-one women, children, and old men who died that night. Maybe it all comes down to that one girl. For her, let there be justice. Let there be justice so her soul can rest in peace—so ours can too.

I was furious upon hearing the first news reports of the story of Kerrey's unit killing women, children, and elderly men. My mind was whiplashed back to the hospital ship. There could never be justification for what had happened to that boy and woman, but here we were again, making excuses. I remember the hypocrisy of talking heads who said if you weren't there, then you couldn't judge Kerrey and then went on to make excuses for him. By his admission, children were brutally killed. And if in the absence of the craziness of war, in dispassionate reason and moral recourse we can't judge, then when can we? That is the very time to do so. To not only judge those acts as wrong then but for all time—then, just maybe, the horrors of Abu Ghraib might have been prevented.

When the court martial for the My Lai massacre was being held, I ran into a woman collecting signatures in front of a grocery store. The petition called for amnesty for Calley. I literally stopped in my tracks. Hot blood pumped in my veins. How could this be? How had we come to the point where war criminals could be excused as long as they wrapped themselves in the flag? How had we lowered ourselves to the hellish depths of the Nazi war criminals, with their excuse that they were merely following orders or that the stress of war made them do evil things? How had we allowed ourselves to embrace evil? What had happened to the ideals that I had been raised to believe in, the ideals that I thought our country stood for? Was it all a lie, a childhood fantasy? Could God forgive or ever forget those trenches with children, women, and babies in them? There were just too many damned questions that tore at my soul. I turned in anger and stormed off when she approached me, something I was to continue to do for a very long time. But I was not alone.

To The Mike Murdys of the World

Santa Barbara Independent, 8-11-02

So, Mike, I see that death made his final call on you. When I first heard the rumors of your demise, I guessed how you would check out. So many of us go out that way. People attribute it to the nightmares that chase us out of sleep and into our waking hours. This is partially true. They also attribute it to the memories of our friends and comrades and the Vietnamese who touched our lives. This also is partially true. For some of us, it is especially the memories of the children who were baptized by the insanity and brutality of that war.

But you and I know another reason. It was in your eyes: the thousand-yard stare. We had seen death yet have somehow eluded his deadly embrace. It's the stare that looks beyond the next bamboo grove, rice paddy, mountain ridge, or trail, searching him out. We know that the silence hides his breath of death: the sudden crack of AK-47s, the soft thump of mortars, the whoosh of RPGs, the scream of rockets, and the whimper of the death rattle.

His image was in the soft downturn of your eyes, as it was the first time I saw him take form in the brilliant red, bellowing burst of napalm, a particularly hideous weapon—Satan's tears. It was the same presence that I felt on the hospital ship, when I witnessed his malignant imprint in those children's eyes. And we experienced him

41

mocking us. We, with the delusions of our thirteen-month tours, as if time and space could outrun him.

Of course he followed us home, tormenting us. His clammy hands lulled us into sweat-drenched dreams and hollow-eyed wakefulness. We heard his cough in the backfire of a car and felt his ice-tipped fingers running down our spines whenever we heard the whimpering choppers. But I see his fiery red eyes in the faceless memories of the war, as I know you did.

You and I both know they're wrong. Vietnam is not behind us. It lives in the mangled bodies of the Vietnamese children, their flesh acting as magnets for the dragon's teeth of unexploded land mines; their tiny, deformed bodies like sponges for Agent Orange. And it lives in the hearts and minds of the veterans—that is, those of us who aren't home when death makes a house call.

Here's to the Mike Murdys of the world. May you find the peace in death that was stolen from you as a young man.

Mike had been an Army tank driver in Vietnam. He told me a story once. As we used to say, he was fresh meat—newly arrived in country—when he was assigned to a tank. Crawling into the driver's seat, he realized it was wet. Looking down, he saw it was covered in the blood from the previous driver. How was he, how was anyone, ever supposed to forget that?

It reminded me of when I returned to my unit after my stay on the hospital ship. I rummaged through discarded supplies to find myself a set of fatigues, flak jacket, helmet, helmet liner, and a Snoopy blanket: everything the well-dressed grunt needed for proper battlefield attire. Eating lunch with others that day, I couldn't help but be aware of bitter stares from two other grunts. Finally my inquisitive stare caught their eye. "The helmet. It belonged to a buddy of ours," one of them began. "He took a bullet in the head." I tore it off and looked at it. The only thing I could see was a small dent; obviously a bullet had not gone through it there. Had their fallen comrade taken a bullet through the face and then it traveled upwards? Or perhaps death came in through the back of his head? I viewed the helmet in a different light after that, no longer secure in the dubious protection that it offered. Just another illusion shattered.

The war came home in other ways as well. Wars always come home in the end. There was a man with a wife and three kids. He was an African-American veteran who used to scare the employees of the Department of Social Services with his angry and bellicose behavior whenever he came into our offices. When he crossed the doors of the agency, the front desk clerks would immediately call me, in near panic, since I was the only one who could talk him down. Our connection crossed racial boundaries. It was a relationship forged in the jungles and mountains of Vietnam, in the darkness of the malignant heart of war.

He was a thin man with pronounced neck veins that bulged whenever he went manic, which was most of the time that I saw him. I could see the madness of the war in his intense eyes and the struggle that he put up trying to outdistance its deathly grasp. Once there came an unexpected clarity to his deep brown eyes. I was unsure if it was insight on how to put the war behind him or if he saw himself on the other side, when his life of pain was finally put to rest.

My heart would break when he went ballistic with his children in tow. Their eyes would widen to the size of saucers with fear and confusion. The look his wife would give him and then me was almost too painful to bear. Her sorrowful eyes seemed to ask, "Why him? You're both combat vets; why him and not you? What did he see, what did he do, that broke him so? Why couldn't it have been you and not him? Why are you relatively normal, while we live in the hellacious backwater tide of that insane war? Why?"

Sometime later I was called to his murder trail. The defense attorney wanted me to testify to an account of my interactions with the dead man. He wanted to exonerate his client, the murderer of my fellow brother-in-arms. He needed to establish the fact that my dead friend had engaged in suicide at the hands of another. I couldn't disagree. The man was killed by that war as surely as if by an NVA soldier, not an American citizen who had pumped him full of lead. His name will never be on the Wall, but it should be. It should be branded in all of our hearts. I often see the eyes of his children and wife floating in the make-believe world for all too many, where truth holds the center against the spin doctors who try to act as the gatekeepers of history.

What Price Glory?

Noozhawk.com, 5-25-09

A Marine vet of the Afghanistan War kills himself rather than face the future, certain that his war memories are forever. The point about how long-term memories of the horror of war linger and fester was driven home when he looked around the rap group and saw Vietnam vets—he just wasn't up to his life being ruled by his nightmarish memories. Something went horribly wrong, as almost everything that is attached to war inevitably does. I think the mistake we make is when we try and convince returning combat vets that it will be otherwise, that somehow the dreams and memories fade with time, or at least lose their horror. It never does, and it never will.

Each combat veteran has his or her own memory of war, the particular incident or incidences that over time become woven into the fabric of their beings, till they can no longer tell where one ends and the other begins. The bitter pain doesn't ever lessen, but it does become familiar and, in an odd way, natural. The memories and nightmares become who you are, and you become them. As time goes by, you find yourself retreating easily and often into that alternative world—one that you share with no one else on this side of the divide. It's a sacred space that you pretend with others that you don't retreat to on a daily—or if lucky, only on a weekly—basis, even decades later.

You find that with time, the people you shared those particular moments with in war become your friends—actually, more than friends, they become your confidantes, family-like—and you hold on dearly to them. They could be the other Marines on a hospital ship or the burnt civilians that you met there but never shared a word with. But communication did happen—it flowed between you and them, regardless of cultural and linguistic differences. They could be the Marines you shared a fighting hole with, while mortars imbedded themselves into Mother Earth and shocked fear into you, while shredding the air with jagged bits of death. These comrades of the nether world didn't even have to be alive at the time of the encounter. They could be the Marine on your ward that died a horrible death by malaria or the sergeant killed in the ambush, the one you carried in a poncho, with his arm dangling and bouncing up and down. You remember how death looked in his eyes—his fear and knowledge of death—and you saw his hopelessness in them, when he realized that there was nothing he could do about it.

Alive and dead, without a word spoken, you share consecrated space with all of them. It's a time and place captured within your soul, peppered with the sounds of death, both personal and impersonal: the terror in men's voices; the hard quietness of the maimed; the cry of full-grown, combat-hardened men reduced to child-like states. It includes the smells of napalm and white phosphorous, of wet decay and fear that populated the land then, as it does that part of your mind now. All the terrible wounds that we inflicted on each other in the name of patriotism or nationalism, but really it was simply driven by fear and hatred. A fear and hatred so primordial and so profoundly overwhelming, so evil, that you find your tongue tied into knots and you stutter into silence when confronted by even the remotest possibility of trying to share its existence with those who have not experienced it.

And yet time and again you retreat to this place—a state of existence where part of you becomes alive only there—that real estate of the mind that you have spent a lifetime building fences around. Alone, without the presence of others, only here can you drop the pretenses that the war was left behind, that you have moved on. Here you accept the harsh reality that you never did and never will. It's not a question of willpower but of what is. You are accepted as who you are, with all falsehoods dropped, part of them as they are of you—that place and time forever frozen within your soul.

At times, the knowledge, the fear, the seduction, that with death, your soul will be pulled back to then, to them, nags at your conscious. That perhaps, just maybe, the forever of purgatory is to be with them in that place. It's the siren song of combat veterans—one that, with time, you find a small part of you welcomes. You have found acceptance—a place where you finally belong. The falsehoods can be dropped as the horror reclaims you—welcomes you—the real welcome home.

CHAPTER SEVEN

There are times when only fiction can reflect the emotional truth, digging for the deeper meanings of the incomprehensible.

"Be Careful What You Bring Back"

Unpublished

Searing pain tore at his chest. The adrenaline rush pumped Wayne's heart to the breaking point. He briefly wondered if an eighteen-year-old could suffer a heart attack? If it wasn't for the crackling fire of AK-47s, the pounding of the artillery, he was sure that he would be able to hear his heart beating into overdrive. As it was, he was hoping that it wouldn't thump free of his chest, bursting forth, looking for escape. He wouldn't blame it; he too was looking for escape.

The incoming whoosh of the RPG gave him a second to lower his head. He felt the warmth of the portable missile of death when it sailed past his head, missing taking it off by inches. Enough of this shit! he told himself, and he dived into the rice paddy on both sides of the trail that he was on. He immediately pushed himself into the muddy trench wall that was holding the water captive, and a barrage of mortars stalked the trail that he had been running on seconds before. How in the hell were they able to see in the dark! It was like the mortars had sensors geared into his personal smell.

Maybe he shouldn't take it so personally. Maybe the cold, impersonal mortars had all their scents—the platoon's, that is: its scent of fear, its scent of guilt. He squeezed his eyes tighter, so tight that tears welled up behind them with so much force that it threatened to pop his eyes free of his skull. Dear God, please, I'll be good from

46

now on—please! Slowly lifting his head from the mud, he sniffed. Smoldering bamboo, smelling a lot like the dry brush that burned yearly in Southern California, was heavy upon the land. He was glad it was night. He didn't want, had no need, to see the burning remains of what had once been a village.

Damn them to hell! Why did they level the village? For what purpose? Lowering his head, he choked back the truth. It wasn't they; it was us, all of us. He knew where he was, back to the nightmare, except this was a waking one. A glimmer of hope was born. That's it, a nightmare. None of this is real. He would wake to find himself back in the world, back in California. But the coldness of the water threatening to cramp his legs cut into that fantasy escape. This was real, as real as his fear was, as real as reality would ever get.

Slowly, as if in a trance, he reached out to the water with his hand. Never again would he find solace and joy in water. He knew surfing was something he would never do again. That is, if he lived past the next few moments.

Scooping up the water, he splashed his face as quietly as he could. Thirst sandblasted his throat raw, reminding him that he had had his last drink hours before, in the midst of a blistering, one hundred twenty-degree day. It was just before the NVA had walked their mortars into the middle of the column, shredding and scattering Marines to hell and back. Cupping water in his hands, he brought them up to drink. But then his hands stalled in mid-action. A tremor ran down his arms. He struggled. He brought them closer; the tremor turned into ongoing shakes. The closer he brought them to his lips, the harder his hands shook. To his surprise, he opened his hands, releasing what was left of the water. The violent tension fled his body along with the water. A cracked smile came to his bloody lips. He couldn't. He wanted to drink but he couldn't. Didn't know why not, but knew it was important not to. Maybe, just maybe the answer had something to do with sin. You were supposed to suffer for doing wrong. He was comfortable with that. That was the way he had been brought up: you paid for your sins. He was about to get real close to this particular comfort zone.

Déjà vu glued itself to his skin as if he had been rolled in cotton candy. In spite of the brown, mucky water that he was partially submerged in, the dread of being here before was sticky and suffocating—like someone or something was trying to rob him of breath. He became light-headed from lack of oxygen. Breathing became even more painful. Please let it not be there. But he knew it would be. Like a junkie drawn to drugs, he was forced to look. Lifting his head, he saw the blackened mound in the flash of a bursting bomb. Was it only the day before that they had set up base camp here? The mound was the top of a shallow bomb shelter where two NVA soldiers had holed up, refusing their one and only request to surrender before they had been tear-gassed, burned by Willey Peter, and incinerated with napalm. Their lieutenant had used them as the excuse to fry the village, turning the inhabitants into crispy critters. Because of two stay-behinds? Two left-behinds? Two deserters?

Wayne sighed and tried to keep his thoughts off his constricting throat. What he wouldn't give for a root beer float. He could feel the ice cream melting in his mouth, satiating his taste buds with sweet vanilla. "Damn that man!"

Wayne looked nervously about. He had spoken out loud. Hadn't meant to, but there it was. He leaned his feverish head against the cold metal of his M16. There was no reason, none at all, for what they had done. He tried escaping into the rational. What could he have done? He was only a private, a grunt, a new guy at that. It was the officer who had made the decision to call in arty and air on the village. It was out of his hands. What could he have done?

But the two dead gooks that fouled the air with their odor was another story: They were the enemy. They deserved to die! As soon as he thought it, he knew it was a lie. His heart told him that violence; the indiscriminate violence of war, any and all wars, was the real enemy. It was a violence that gave birth to fear, which in turn became corrosive and ate away at his heart. He might be a new guy, but he knew that turning people's houses into burnt chambers of death was wrong: That the killing of men, women, and children, even the killing of the so-called enemy, was wrong. After all, what made them the enemy? Speeches by old men safely encased in capitals of the world, another reality removed? The fact that they had taken up a gun to defend family and community from such violence as had been visited upon this village?

In thirty years, would they still be the enemy? Would anyone care about them or what happened here? Or would they simply be forgotten, replaced by others: enemy of the day, much like an ice cream flavor of the month?

Rapid movement from down the rice paddy disturbed his thoughts, along with the water. Water sloshed, sounding like the heavy waves at the Wedge back in California. He suddenly realized that the mortars and the crack of enemy rifles had stopped. And it had been a long time since he had heard Marine M16s coughing back. No, not enemy rifles. No more! The only enemy he had, he decided, was the violence of war. Still, he swung his M16 around, ready to cut loose a barrage of death. The sound came closer, sending ripples lapping at his waist. Bringing his rifle up he dug it hard into his shoulder as a crouching silhouette approached. He tightened his finger on the trigger and tasted the cold sweat that tickled his upper lip. Then his father's words rang out, loud in the night: "The war will last thirteen months for you, son; survive that. Then you must live with your conscience for the rest of your life. Be careful what you do, what you bring back with you, so you can survive that. That's the hard part." When Wayne had first heard his father tell him that, he assumed he basically meant the first part of the statement. Now, he knew better. "Be careful what you bring back." Guilt was a bitch! Lowering his rifle, he remembered how sad his dad had been when he enlisted.

His old man had served in the Corps in the Pacific during World War II. He never understood why his dad didn't share war stories with him, like some of the other kids' fathers had. He remembered his dad's disgust with those who had served safely in the rear and told the bravest, fondest stories of war. He was beginning to understand his dad for the first time: his intensity, the depths of his sorrow. He lowered his rifle, letting it slip from his hands into the water. He hadn't consciously meant to, but there it was.

A body fell on him. A grunt, a soft curse; an American curse.

"Who? Who is it?" Wayne whispered hoarsely, his throat hurting with the effort.

"Who is it? What kind of challenge is that?"

Wayne went stone cold. It was the lieutenant's voice.

A loud explosion threw dirt high. The light revealed the man cringing next to Wayne. His expression was wild: his lips pulled tightly back, eyes flaring wide open, whitewashed skin aging him considerably beyond his twenty-seven years. He held a .45 tightly to his chest.

"Are you wounded?" the lieutenant whispered in the excruciating quiet that followed explosions.

"No."

"What's your name?"

"Surfer."

"Surfer? Your name, numb nuts, not those stupid nicknames you give each other."

"Surfer." Wayne was surprised, then delighted, that he no longer wanted to claim any other identity than the nickname that had followed him from boot camp. It was his way of divorcing himself from the insanity that surrounded him.

"Does a rank come with that?" the lieutenant asked sarcastically. "What's that ungodly smell?" he asked in his clipped speech, sniffing the air.

"Your work," Wayne replied.

"My work?"

"The smell of rotten eggs? That would be white phosphorous— Willey Peter, as we call it. You know, not even water will put it out. It'll burn right through a human body—from one side clear to the other."

"What the hell are you talking about?"

"And the other smell, the acrid one, is fried human flesh. And of course, then there's the smell of the toasted village. God know how many crispy critters you made there."

"Are you nuts? Shell-shocked? Don't think so, so give it a rest. A Section 8 won't do you any good out here."

Silence crept into the paddy. In some ways it was worse than the noise of rifle fire and the loud explosions of bombs going off.

"You've seen anyone else?"

"Anyone else? You mean us? Them? The villagers? The two guys ..."

"What the hell's the matter with you? What are you babbling about?"

"Death?"

"Death?"

The moon breaking free from the clouds cast a brilliant white light. The lieutenant looked askance at Wayne.

"Where's your rifle?"

"Lost it."

"Lost it? You are one for the books. How about a canteen? Got any water left?"

"Nope."

"Figures." The officer took his own canteen out and began to unscrew it. He submerged it into the black water. Bubbles gently filled the night air. Bringing it up, he poured half it down his throat before coming up for air. "Want some?" he asked, offering the canteen to Wayne.

Panic welled up in Wayne. He vigorously shook his head no.

"Thought you didn't have a canteen? When did you last have a drink?"

"Long time," came the garbled reply.

"Then have some!" the lieutenant commanded, pushing the canteen hard at Wayne.

"No! Be careful what you bring back!"

"What are you babbling about now?"

When Wayne refused to answer, the lieutenant pushed himself up to the bank's edge and peaked over. "Damn them gooks!"

Even though the man had whispered his curse, Wayne recoiled like he had shouted it. Never before had he heard, really heard, how awful the word sounded. In shame he relived the moment minutes before when he had said the word within the confines of his skull. If war was the problem, then racism was the tool that allowed men to dehumanize each other so they could kill each other as abstracts, not as flesh and blood, with souls attached. His chin dropped. He had a lot to learn—that is, unlearn. He had a lot of soul cleansing to do.

"Goddamn them gooks, they killed my men!" This time the words were spoken louder.

"And you, that is, us, them." Wayne's words were mere whispers.

"What?" the lieutenant said, sliding down. Wayne heard the click when the officer took the safety off his .45.

"Don't you see? We kill them because they kill us. And they kill us because we kill them. It's savagery, plain and simple." Swallowing hard, he continued. "Why do you invoke God's name?"

"Because he would want us to kill them bastards!"

"Really? What about the first commandment? The very first commandment."

"They're godless communists! They aren't Christians! We're doing his work here."

"Thou shall not kill. It does not say thou shall not kill only Christians."

Wayne could feel his life being weighed on some inner scale by the officer. In time he heard the click. The safety was back on. An easier breath came to him.

"Perhaps we need to be quiet or risk giving our position away," Wayne suggested, having no death wish to press his luck. Besides, everything was said that needed to be said. "I suggest we wait here for morning and pray to God the company mounts a rescue mission."

The lieutenant tensed and took another hard pull from his canteen. Mercifully, Wayne heard no more from the officer that night. Time seemed to have taken a step sideways. He tried to figure out what to tell his dad, but nothing that would make sense came to him. Finally, near morning, calmness settled over him. That was it! There was nothing to say. Like his dad, he would have no war stories to glorify hell and beguile those who had never tasted its bitter taste.

He must have literally passed out from exhaustion, thirst, and adrenaline overload. The sound of the lieutenant drinking water and stirring brought him back into the immediate present. Bright sunlight broke the horizon. He cocked his head to one side when the sound of approaching helicopters demanded his attention. The lieutenant stood cautiously and looked about. All was as quiet as a morgue. The noise of the rescue choppers grew louder, till a flight of them streaked overhead. Either for good measure or for the joy of killing, they let loose with a barrage of rocket and machine gun fire. The officer smiled, stretched, and climbed up the muddy embankment.

He stood like a proud peacock, with his .45 firmly grasped in one hand and a partially empty canteen dangling from the other. He turned back to face Wayne, who saw the lieutenant's boastful smile turn to horror. First the pistol dropped, and then the canteen crashed down to earth. The man dropped to his knees. Dry heaves wracked his body. Wayne stood, his face soft and questioning. He turned, his eyes drawn to the far end of the small rice patty. His questioning look became deeper. He had no idea that human remains could decompose so fast, even in the humid conditions of Vietnam. The dozen or so bodies bobbing in the water were grotesquely bloated, with blackened skin. They were in transition, somewhere between a solid and liquid state.

"Be careful what you bring back." A wounded look took over Wayne's face. He now had his war story for those who insisted on the glory and honor of war. And the lieutenant? He had a war souvenir that would remain a part of him as long as he lived.

Vietnam: The War That Keeps on Giving and Giving ...

The wars against the homeless continue, as does yet another foreign misadventure overseas: Iraq. The ghost of Vietnam echoes in the streets with each fresh nightly news broadcast, with each new death. Frequently they merge, so that it seems as if one war collapses into the other. Perhaps this was best illustrated this year for me by the next story.

Rumors of War Are Never-Ending

Unpublished

The bright sun bounced harshly off the white sandy beach, so at first I did not see the tears in Keith's eyes. But I knew something was wrong from the way he looked down, immobilized, his gaze captured by a single cross. Looking around, I saw others behaving the same way, and I understood. They were seeing a single cross in the field of crosses, one for each American military man or woman killed in Iraq. It was Memorial Day, 2005. We were at Arlington West in

Santa Barbara, where locals honored and grieved for those killed in yet another war. For Keith, the war had come home. It had become personal. Against my better judgment I approached him and asked what the trouble was. With a scratchy voice, he replied, "It's my nephew."

My gaze was drawn to a woman who sat a little further down. She had brought her own candles with her. She was in her mid-forties, with shoulder-length dark hair. The blouse she wore bore a photo of her son, who had recently been killed in Iraq. Her vacant stare belonged to another time, perhaps when she had held her baby son in her arms. Now her arms hung loosely at her side, lifeless, as dead to the world as her son. My insides went cold, and a painful knot formed in my stomach. I thought, Again? We have to go through this again? Shane, my eleven-year-old son, slid his hand into mine; possibly he saw the pain in my eyes. Perhaps he was reflecting on the pain of all the dead represented by the simple white wooden crosses.

Days before, while making my rounds in the early morning hours, I had stopped by a group of homeless men. They were boisterous, their comradely joking fueled by booze. We exchanged friendly barbs and slaps on the back while I gently inquired as to their condition. Out of the corner of my eye, I watched one man, who did not engage in the by now familiar banter of the streets. "We have something in common," he finally said, having caught my stare.

The group grew quiet. I knew what he meant. We were both Vietnam veterans. There was an ache in the man's voice that demanded my full attention. One of the other men coughed nervously; another emitted an audible groan.

"A cop stopped me yesterday morning with a phone number. Said it was important to call. So I did. The voice on the other end said they'd been trying to reach me—to tell me my son is dead, killed in Iraq."

I expressed my sorrow for his loss, for his pain. We all stood silent for a moment, and then I walked away.

I had a client once; I met him one day at a soup kitchen. He had the longest, bushiest beard I had ever seen in my life. In sharp contrast, his shiny bald head reflected the rays of the sun. His faded and torn jungle camouflage uniform reflected his homeless veteran status. Like me, he had come back from Vietnam more or less in one piece. Unlike me, he had headed for the hills and then the streets, where he was to live with his memories for the next twenty years. In Santa Barbara, he found a small community that afforded him respect and a small degree of peace. Not letting go of his memories, he was able to move off the streets when he learned to co-exist with them.

I have a friend who was likewise nearly destroyed by memories. In Vietnam, he had carried the skull of an enemy soldier around in his backpack for months. How the man had died and how the skull was separated from the rest of his body and from its brain and flesh, I never asked. In many ways, my friend never did let go of that skull. It haunts him day and night. It literally drove him crazy. My friend hated the war. Only those who made excuses for the war would draw more of his ire.

Keith was also a Vietnam veteran. He has his own memories, as do I. Now Keith has a new war, a new reason for mind-bending memories. This war has awakened all the old, bitter memories, reopened all the old, caustic wounds. Somehow, it seems only right that a person should have to deal with only one war in a lifetime. But now, like an un-expected storm that steals in with the night, clouds of war have begun to slip back into our communities. The pain and insanity that is the calling card of war have begun to infiltrate our cities and towns again.

The body counts go higher, the suffering of the innocent bleeds in our souls, and the pain of those who serve is only now beginning to be felt. In thirty years, the veterans of this war will write articles expressing the age-old disgust combat soldiers share for war. They will write of those who died on the battlefields and those who succumbed once they got home.

Maybe somewhere along the line, war will skip a generation. Maybe if that happens, just maybe, then the evil that gives birth to war will wither, much like a plant that goes without water. Maybe at that time all these bitter memories can slip quietly into the night. Until then, I approach each person I run into with guarded apprehension, wondering: Does he have a new rumor of war?

Ken Williams

Unnecessary Heroes

Santa Barbara Independent, 9-16-06
For those of us who have served in war, the unrelenting bad news from Iraq carries a bitter, yet familiar, ring. Not only the mounting Marine and army casualties and the tens of thousands of civilians killed but also the heart-wrenching news of Americans being accused of wartime atrocities. We close our eyes and hear the footsteps of Vietnam. In the silence, we feel the hot breath of evil that war gives birth to. Again we taste the fear, hear the cries of the wounded, and see the accusing stares of the dead. Again we find Americans being accused of the most vile and hideous crimes, and we know; the evilness of war, war the monstrous entity, is once again unleashed upon the world.

Through Democratic and Republican administrations, the only constant is war. In my own lifetime it was first the Asian wars in Laos, Cambodia, and Vietnam in the name of anti-communism. Millions dead, including fifty-six thousand Americans, and what was the result of all that hatred? The genocidal Khmer Rouge and a countryside devastated by chemicals, as if Dow Chemical and other multinationals had declared war on nature itself. Vietnamese children by the thousands were and are deformed by Agent Orange, as are the children of veterans who fought there. And if that wasn't enough, Vietnamese children continue to be maimed and killed by leftover bombs and mines. And lest we forget, hundreds of thousands of American veterans were psychologically and spiritually damaged and sentenced to lifetimes of homelessness.

Then a decade later, again in the name of anti-communism, war came to Central America. The government, our government, found the work of the death squads a necessity and a Contra war a must, leaving hundreds of thousands dead and more bearing the marks of torture.

Now, in the name of security, we kill, again, invoking our God against their God. How did we come to naively believe that a tortured country, ruled by a mad dictator could find war an antidote? How can replacing the straightjacket of a dictatorship with car bombings, death squads, torture, random murder, mayhem, religious intolerance, and hatred make the world a safer place? Of course, war doesn't. What the Iraq war has done is give birth to a new generation of terrorists. For every action there is a reaction.

The humiliation of the embassy crisis in Iran in the 1980s was set in motion in the 1950s, when the CIA orchestrated the overthrow of their democratically elected government in the name of big oil. The cowardly attack on the Twin Towers was done by some of the same people we used, and allied with to fight the Soviet invasion of Afghanistan. And now we put American boys in the midst of a religious conflict dating back hundreds of years, in the middle of a society where our religion, our speech, our colors of skin and way of life all mark us as the enemy.

And speaking of God, when did he/she get hijacked by those who hate? By intolerant people who find hatred in their hearts for people different than themselves, be it sexual preference, other religious beliefs, or the "enemy"? When are we going to liberate God from the prejudices and hatred some people put on him? When can God be God and not a tool for someone's agenda?

As in Vietnam, the atrocities committed today speak to the reality of unending war, of fragile young minds and spirits being bent and then broken by the hideous sights and sounds of war. Violence, and war is nothing but violence concentrated and intensified to its purist form, will always claim its due. Who among the war's cheerleaders will be there ten or twenty years down the road, when returning veterans find the cold streets of our country are their payback? Who will be there to cradle them in their arms when the flashbacks and nightmares claim their due?

Give our founding fathers their due. They saw a world engulfed in war, with militarized states growing with each new conflict, and decided we need not be a part of that. Give Dr. King credit, the saintly man who reminded us that violence, regardless of the cause it serves, always ends up mutating, bending and destroying those who engage in it.

Stop the slaughter. Let at least one generation of Americans grow up without tasting the bitterness of war. Let us once again lead by our ideals and not by the terror of our weapons. Those in Washington want others to fear us, not like or respect us. Fear does not lead to a better tomorrow. Fear leads to hatred of thy neighbor and to a world drenched in blood. We knew that at one time. We need to return to our idealism and common sense.

If anything, war taught me that there is such a thing as evil. It has shape and form as much as love and the very air we breathe do. Unlike love, evil needs critical mass to come truly alive, and war is its natural and perfected breeding ground. Men, and now women, do things they would never do otherwise. They become monsters and torturers, only to wake up once they come home to the terrible knowledge of what they did. Some break with that knowledge, while others become bent with the joy of killing and lording over others. But most of us simply find ways to struggle on: to spend a lifetime trying to overcome what war does to us but never really leaving the war behind. We, forever, till the day we die, live with one foot in the present and one foot in the past: the brotherhood of arms.

Book Two

Santa Barbara's
Homeless Wars

CHAPTER EIGHT

I came home from war and went to school. I also did political work—against the war and for farm workers, political prisoners, renter's rights, just about any progressive cause that would buy off my conscience. It was all good work but did nothing to alleviate my painful memories. Like Mike, Vietnam was always there, lurking in the shadowy corners, waiting for the unexpected loud noise or the sound of choppers, filling the air with the hypnotic, rhythmic sound of churning blades. At times I was crippled by intrusive thoughts, invasive feelings, by a sense of danger in a crowd or alone on a street, in the way I needed to sit in a public restaurant facing the entrance. There was always a reason to remember ...

I moved to Santa Barbara in the early 1970s, attended college, graduated, and then got a job at the Department of Social Services; I added union organizing to my credentials. I negotiated ten contracts on behalf of welfare and probation workers and led the most successful strike against the county in its history. And then I fell into my destiny, or fulfilled it, with my career of working with the homeless. I did not so much select my calling in life as it chose me.

Thirty-some odd years ago, while working in the Aid for Families with Dependent Children program, better known as AFDC, or welfare for poor families, I came across a mother and two children living out of their car. Not only was the sadness of the children present in their mother's eyes but also a disconnection, caused by either mental illness or emotional trauma of some type. It was winter, and darkness had fallen early and easily. This was before the streets of America became flooded with homeless children, so it was still quite a shock for me to deal with a family that had no place to go for the evening. It was also a time before shelters mushroomed across the land.

The visual image implanted in my brain of that evening at work is of the woman and her two children sitting on the floor behind my desk while I searched frantically for a place for them to stay. A tortured part of my memory is the fact that I can't remember the outcome of that night. I remember other workers in the unit casting questioning looks at them, then at me. They were as baffled by the situation as I was: homeless families in rich Santa Barbara? The subtle signs of the mother's mental illness and the oddness of them sitting on the floor, combined with me allowing them into our office, traditionally off-limits for clients, all contributed to the surreal atmosphere that evening. The mystical bond between them and me that had developed so rapidly was readily apparent but impossible to categorize. All of this was new territory, unfortunately one that was to become all too familiar. But what became of them? There have been just too many families in crisis since that time in the seventies. Their faces and all their pain runs together into a collage of mad, modern abstract art, disjointed lives joined together by overarching despair. Thousands of homeless families and homeless children have slipped through my hands since then, some with solutions that worked, some with tragedies as outcome.

Soon after that encounter with my first homeless family, I transferred into the General Relief Unit. GR, as it was called on the streets, is welfare for single, unattached adults, though I continued to work with families in the shelters. GR was the gateway for me to the streets just when the homeless crisis was rearing its head. Little did I know at that time that the streets were becoming the focal point for yet another war; this time, the war was against the homeless.

Within the department, GR had a rogue connotation. At that time it was a cash aid program that basically dealt with street alcoholics and what was left of the street culture of the fifties and early sixties. This nuance was to change radically, practically overnight. All other welfare programs had either federal or state monies, with rules and regulations attached to them. GR had neither, being entirely funded, operated, and designed by the county. Unfortunately, this resulted in a lot of fast and loose operations that were questionably legal, such as allowing only two weeks of benefits per year for those deemed employable (which in itself was a questionable and evasive category to begin with), and then only if the recipient got housing first. As a GR worker, I would hand a housing form to the potential client, who then took it to a welfare hotel. If the manager signed it, the department would grant benefits; if not, no application was given and no record of the agency's interactions with the client was ever taken or recorded.

When I first transferred into GR, another practice was to engage in Greyhound Therapy in conjunction with the Department of Mental Health whenever possible. The DMH would shoot the client/ patient full of thorazine, a nasty and extremely potent anti-psychotic medicine (one with terrible side effects). They would then bring the person over, have him or her sign an application, and we would in turn write out a bus ticket. Either Mental Health or GR staff would then drive the client/patient to the bus station and literally pour the poor soul onto the bus.

I remember the first time I participated in this. A Mental Health Department car pulled up in our parking lot—literally at the back door. The patient was so overly medicated that the two staff persons accompanying him had to hold him up. I laid out the application on the hood of the car. Thorazine is not only an extremely powerful anti-psychotic medication but also a heavy-duty muscle relaxant. It was known in the field as a "chemical straightjacket." The poor man was unable to control his tongue muscles, so it hung out of his mouth and down to his chin. His pants were too big, so he tried hanging onto them with hands that refused to work. To sign the application for benefits, the Mental Health staff member placed the pen in his hand, closed a hand over his, and helped (forced) him to sign his name: For what purpose? To make the facade somehow legitimate or to buy off our consciences?

I had been there before and sure as hell was not going to live with the pain of that guilt again. Soon thereafter, I made my way to a poverty law center, and a series of lawsuits followed that was to sanitize the more odorous practices of the agency.

Of course the agency suspected my part in the lawsuits. One time one of the bosses was giving a tour to two of the lead attorneys from the poverty center. When she brought them into the GR Unit, she introduced them to all the other staff but me. Finally turning to me, she said, "And I believe you already know them, being that they are such good friends of yours."

No retaliation ever came my way, either because management knew the practices were wrong or because of my leadership in the union. For several years the successful strike that I had led as the president of the union gave me breathing room for homeless advocacy.

And then the AIDS crisis hit. I had read in the newspapers about the Gay Plague, as it was at first called. It was a mysterious disease of biblical proportions, without a known infectious route but seemingly linked to blood. But what else was it connected to? What other ways could one get it?

AIDS was the perfect disease, a killer, a so-called retribution plague that spoke to ingrained prejudices. Talk of quarantining infected people was widely heard. Hysteria stalked the land. Fear led the charge to curtail sick people's civil rights, and politicians played games with their lives. Across the country children were barred from school, and many adults lost their jobs and livelihoods. Still many more became social outcasts, lepers in their own communities.

I knew it was only a matter of time before I came into contact with it. I played it over and over again in my mind: what would I do? How would I react? Would my humanity or my fear win? Which one would triumph? The hysteria within the agency was insidious and contagious, mirroring the broader society.

It happened as it often does. The stark decision comes in a split second, forcing your hand—reach out and embrace your humanity or give in to your fears and run away. He was middle-age and gay, typical of a man with AIDS at the beginning of the plague. He had the open sores, the wasting away—shedding pounds before your eyes—along with the early onset of dementia when the disease attacked the brain. It was typical only in retrospect. Then, it was all terrifyingly new.

I had taken an application from him and given it to my unit clerk to set up the case. She gingerly gave it back to me, holding it by the corner with two fingers. "You set it up," she told me. The next day he came in to show me a letter. Social Security needed him to call. I took him back to the unit and let him use my phone. The other workers gave me strange looks and a wide berth.

The next day was my scheduled day off. Upon my return, tension was readily apparent in the unit. No one would look at me, and no one spoke. Settling in at my desk, I noticed that I had been given a new phone. I was happy at first, but then a dense awareness set in. "Why a new phone?" I asked. The story dribbled reluctantly out. My coworkers had complained to management about me allowing my client who was suffering from AIDS to use the phone. Management in turn had called the phone company. A man with elbow-long rubber gloves showed up, bagged my phone in plastic, tightly taped it, and took it away to bury it in a landfill.

Conflicting emotions ensued: The image that sprang to mind of a man decked out in a HAZMAT suit was amusing. The connotation of such naked fear and prejudice was chilling to the bone.

The next time I saw the client in question, his condition had deteriorated greatly. Getting up from a chair to leave, he staggered as a wave of disequilibrium cut his legs out from under him. The decision was being forced. I reached out and held him in a firm grasp. Sweat broke freely on his face as he held on for dear life. A weak smile came to his pale face next. We both looked deeply into the abyss that for a brief moment was peeled back. He was dying alone from some unknown, terrible disease. Yet the same disease had allowed me to lay claim to part of my humanity, something that I was afraid I might have lost in Vietnam. Gathering his strength, he let go of me. His soulful eyes said it all: they thanked me for not shirking away from his touch. Like hundreds of my clients over the years, he shuffled away to die.

Crack was to join AIDS in the eighties and nineties; together those two epidemics were to cut through the homeless in Santa Barbara like a tsunami, as it did throughout the country. John Jamieson, the director of the local Salvation Army and a saint in our community, asked me to go over my notes and come up with a list of those who had recently died on our street. The plan was to put their names on plaques on a wall to honor their passing. We also hoped that it would serve as an educational tool in the streets about the dangers of unprotected sex, shared needle use, and the devastating consequences of alcohol and drug use in general.

But we also had another population in mind to educate: the citizens of Santa Barbara. In our naivety and idealism, we hoped, assumed, and prayed that this wall would shock citizens out of their complacency and that they in turn would demand that the government take steps to end this local, state, and national shame.

Actually sitting down and remembering all those who had died was a chilling experience. Like in war, weekly casualty lists became the norm. People are only moved when the baseline death rate suddenly skyrockets. To sit and stare at a list of dead clients and friends, the people whom I spent more time with than my family, became an overwhelming and extremely sad experience. Judging from my own feelings, I was sure that John and I had stumbled upon the perfect solution to the benign apathy that was killing so many.

In time, more memorial walls followed that first endeavor. Within a year, the board had to be doubled; so many people were dying on our streets. The last name we put on it was Linda Archer, a homeless woman brutally murdered.

Linda

Unpublished

Linda didn't look homeless. Her eyes were clear, not filmed with an overlay of alcohol nor colored with the manic intensity or fright of the mentally ill. Her neatly trimmed brown hair hung free down to her shoulders and softly encased her oval face. Her clothes were always cleaned and neatly pressed. In the shelters she always sat in the last row or vacant chair, causing no fuss, drawing no attention her way. She was the type of woman who would easily blend into the fabric of middle-class existence. If riding the bus, a person might take a quick second glance her way and see no hint of her homeless status. But upon closer inspection, not all was well. Her lips never turned up in a smile. Her eyes were always on guard, as if she expected trouble around the next corner. And in her ordinariness, her lack of acting-out behavior was in itself a clue. She just didn't belong in the shelters, sitting day after day, week after week, month after month, never going anywhere, never keeping appointments of any kind, never asking for help from the outreach workers who flowed in and out of the shelters like the tide. In the end she did keep one appointment: an appointment with Death. Death masqueraded as a scumbag who paid a visit to her homeless camp next to the freeway. Death came, brutal and ugly. In the end she was just another statistic to the city, another unsolved murder, another death among the homeless, to be filed away and forgotten. But for those of us who managed to finally exchange a fleeting glance with her, a burning, hurting mystery lingers, not only about the identity of her cowardly murderer but of the tragic life that this poor woman lived and how her visit to the streets of Santa Barbara would end up causing her death.

She was to be our last honoree on the wall, because we said we didn't have the money to buy the five-dollar plaques and wood to expand it time after time. The more personal reason was because it was just too painful. We had lost our battle with apathy, and to see our friends adding their wasted lives to the wall seemed meaningless.

I began to keep journals of the streets at about the same time. In particular, and especially in the beginning, I focused on those who had died. I started to do this out of a sense of shame and guilt when I realized I had begun to forget some of my clients and friends. Faces and stories had begun to blend together in a blur. And I didn't want to dishonor them by forgetting.

To forget would also have been a crime, an admission that those in society and government who adhered to the philosophy of benign neglect were correct; that is, if we ignored the casualties on the streets, then the issue would eventually fade away—or die, along with the last homeless person. I began to see that I had an important role to play by not letting their deaths, and thus their lives, go unnoticed. If the homeless died by the score, then Santa Barbara would have to accept the moral consequences, because these people were real, not cold, abstract statistics.

There is now a third Wall of Death. One of the true unsung saints of Santa Barbara, a man who wishes to remain in the background, even after giving hundreds of thousands of dollars and hundreds of his personal hours to aid the homeless, had an artist inscribe the names of those who died, which I had collected over the years in my journals, on a brick wall in a meeting hall that he owned. He did this to honor their passing, to honor them so someone would always know about this debacle and also know of the real men, women, and babies who fell victim to the street wars at home. To stand before this wall with over two hundred and fifty names on it is a truly moving experience. The feeling is one much like I had when I stood before the moving wall of the Vietnam Memorial: A mixture of competing and lacerating emotions churned, twisted, and inflicted pain; the overriding one is waste. So much waste of so precious a gift: life.

The Bonds of Friendship

noozhawk.com, 4-14-10

One goes through life meeting people, becoming friends with some. Looking back, the structures of the bonds of friendship can sometimes become clear only with the passage of time. And sometimes those bonds run so deep that they touch and become a part of the very core of who you are. This kind of friendship is like breathing—it is so natural that you end up taking that friendship for granted, yet you cannot imagine life without it. But then something happens; you slow down, look inside, and realize that magical connection.

Chuck, a close friend of mine, approached me years ago with an idea. He wanted to honor those who died on our streets without shelter. They mostly died alone, sometimes unknown—bodies without names but not without souls, a crucial distinction that my friend recognized. He also knew that somewhere they had families and friends, people who loved them and would miss them after their passing.

Chuck recognized that in many ways they were the outcasts of our society—the invisibles. He had noticed that many citizens of our community pass the homeless on our streets without seeing them—knowing what they think they know about them without understanding. And he realized that other members of our community only saw the homeless through eyes filtered by fear.

It bothered him greatly that the invisibles should pass from life the way that they had lived life—without recognition, without the honor that was due them as human beings. So he asked me to come up with a list from my journals of those who had died on our streets. Taking that list, he commissioned a talented local artist, Margaret Matson, to paint their names on a series of white bricks that would become a memorial wall in a large meeting room. She chose magical paint that comes into and out of clarity depending on where your point of view is. It reflects the way we see the homeless on our streets, through irrational fears and prejudices or a moral compass that sees all of us as brothers and sisters.

That was years ago. Ever since, I hand over another list every few months. Every few months Margaret gets her paints ready and records the sadness. But she also tells another story in doing so. This is one of love, of one man reaching out his hand to an outcast group of people. Another man once kept a list that paid homage to his moral belief in the middle of hell. Schindler did what his conscience dictated that he must. In his own way, with another list, my friend commissioned a wall that stands as a bright needle on a compass of compassion.

Often when I am sitting in that room, my gaze will be drawn to the wall. Inevitably it lands on Joshua, the four-month-old baby, the youngest on the wall. Sometimes it lands on the name of the man whose body was found in his camp along 101. I remember driving home that night; it was winter, light rain casting an ominous ambiance. I saw the police and paramedic cars with their red lights slashing through the darkness and knew another homeless body had been found. Sometimes my sight drifts to the man without a leg who died next to his wheelchair. There are so many names— so many friends.

At other times I can hear the muted voices of the dead as they communicate with those they had ended up bordering on the wall, brick to brick—strangers in life, comrades in death. Sometimes they converse with the new members added to that final community of theirs: How did they end up here? What went wrong with their lives? Some share the cruelties of mental illness—a disease some attach a lot of prejudice and fear and not a little hatred to. Sometimes the collected voices reflect the delusions that drive the disease. At other times they speak with the voice of sorrow of love, families, and friends lost because of their untreated sickness, of being outcasts and sentenced to a life of loneliness because of that cruel disease. And I can't help but think of the hundreds that will be abandoned because of the cuts to Mental Health Services; I know that we will need a lot more bricks and a ton of paint when that comes to pass.

"Larry" was one of the homeless with mental issues. How could it be otherwise? He was standing on the other side of the car from his mother when the big rig plowed into her. Racing around the car, he found his mother dead, and his mind snapped. He never recovered from that tragedy till the day he fell and hit his head and finally rejoined his mother. Only then did the nightmares that used to scare him so badly finally cease.

There are so many Larrys on our streets—so many already untreated, and now I fear more will be added to the memorial wall. Yes, we will need a lot more bricks and a lot more paint. We could use a few more caring people like my friend—a few more angels, like he is.

Community Kitchen Update

The Community Kitchen is a bright example of the community reaching out to those in need; it has fed the hungry for the last twenty years. Over three hundred volunteers from twenty different congregations, including All Saints by the Sea; Saint Anthony; S.B. Parish; Old Mission; Free Methodist; Trinity Episcopal; Goleta Presbyterian; Church of Jesus Christ LD; and El Montecito Presbyterian Church, among others, served 70,865 lunches last year to our community. This organization and these people live their faith. Doing so, they add a value to our community that will never be measured by dollars but is priceless nonetheless. It is a moral imperative that they not be forced to shut down, curtail services, or relocate. Let us not forget that we are in the midst of the Great Recession, with fifteen million of our fellow citizens cruelly thrown out of work.

As time progressed and our inability to deal with homelessness showed us how impotent we were before this tragedy, our feelings began to turn to shame. And then some turned that shame into anger and showed prejudicial rage against the homeless, as if somehow it had become their very own personal life task to rain on our parade of life. In Santa Barbara in years past, as in other communities throughout the land, there were stories that some merchants sprinkled bleach and even more powerful chemicals on top of garbage to deter the homeless from rummaging through trash bins, looking for discarded, rotting food. Then there was the year someone began to put ground glass into bottles of wine and placed them around town, hoping some wino deep into addiction would drink it and cut his or her stomach to pieces. I typed out and photocopied a warning, passed the copies out, and posted them in the shelters. But still the horrors kept coming.

One of the most tragic events was the brutal knifing of Michael Stephenson, a twenty-nine-year-old homeless man who had his throat cut in 1985 while he slept peacefully in a park. He elegantly pleaded for his life, telling his killers, "No, my friend, no." Another tragedy was the vicious murder of Luis Altmark in another park, kicked to death by some kids. Beatings of the homeless became too numerous to count. Up the coast in Santa Cruz, they even gave it a name all its own: Troll Hunting. Stories of homies being set on fire came up from LA, along with vicious beatings by men with bats. Then a homeless man set on fire in northern Santa Barbara County struck closer to home. It seemed as if a bounty had been placed on the heads of the homeless. But none of these perps, these haters, needed to have gone to such effort; death comes, casual and fast, to those without homes, without shelter from nature and the human condition.

CHAPTER NINE

I began to write letters to the newspapers somewhere in the 1980s in response to the new war at home: the war against the homeless. Santa Barbara, like the rest of the country, awoke one day to find its streets occupied by a foreign army, the most visible and frightening-seeming of them being the mentally ill; the most tragic were the children. And the reaction of far too many citizens was that "foreigners" were among us, somehow threatening their existences, reminding them of dark things that lurk in the night and bump up against ancient prejudices and fears.

In hindsight it is easy to see the social, economic, and political forces at play that all but made this tragedy inevitable. First were the well-intended but devastating closures of state mental hospitals. The conservative tide in state governments made sure that social programs that should have been there to house and treat the discharged mental patients were instead gutted. As local governmental resources dried up, city councils and county boards of supervisors saw an easy target for budget cuts. After all, who would be crazy enough to throw their lot in with the mentally ill homeless?

Men's flight from commitment and the Age of Divorce made sure that children by the hundreds of thousands would join the internal exile of the dispossessed. The tragedy of America's apparently unending wars produced wave upon wave of disabled vets who found that their experiences in war made them unable to fit into the internal New World Order.

The federal retreat from subsidized housing, welfare cuts, outsourcing of domestic well-paying jobs, to be replaced with minimum wage ones, if at all—all conspired to produce a subgroup, an underclass that no longer had a stake in, nor relationship with, the rest of society.

And in turn society turned on these victims, casting them as the cause rather than the effect of homelessness. Add the overlay of drugs and always reliable alcohol that could cushion the pain and isolation, salve for the bleeding souls of the turned out and abused, to contribute deadly, genocidal-like consequences on large proportions of the homeless. At times it felt like an army of chemists was hard at work to create the next wonder drug, which produced nirvana-like states while destroying bodies and minds at ever-accelerating rates of speed.

And, inevitably, Death strode onto this playing field. Sensing a new opportunity, a new game for his macabre hunt, he descended upon the homeless like the vulture that he is.

In Memory of Twenty-Two

Noozhawk.com, 1-27-08

Dawn breaks cold and blistery. Clouds colored gray with arctic breath lazily drift by, without care. The coffee is hot in my hand, strong and with a bite. I exhale with trepidation, breathe in courage, and look back on 2007 as it finds its resting place in history. The power elite in Washington will gather soon to hear the president go over his state of the union. They will display concern over the economy and the war in Iraq but otherwise congratulate each other on a job well done. But how does the state of the union look to the homeless on the streets, especially those who are mentally or chemically impaired and are forced to live their Dante existence there?

As I look over my journal, I sadly count twenty-two deaths, a truly startling figure for a community this size. But beyond numbers is the reality of each death—of individuals, not just sterile stats, whose lives ended on the cold and unforgiving streets before their time.

Foremost among them is the death of John Doe II, or Darth Vader, as many knew him. A deaf mute, he was famous for the welding mask he wore that completely covered his face. He was a fixture in Santa Barbara and Goleta for more years than I care to remember. He was a very secretive man. With a weary smile I remember how I once stumbled upon his clandestine campsite. Sitting down with

73

him, my eyes suddenly teared. He smelled heavily of smoke, telling me he had camped in the burn area behind the Department of Social Services right after the Painted Cave fire. He was tragically killed while walking on the railroad tracks, unable to hear the approaching train—or was he? Was his tormented life just too painful to continue the struggle? Three other homeless people likewise found their lives cut short by crushing tons of railroad steel. As usual in such situations, low voices questioned the real cause of death, as stories of the pain that each one endured were bantered about.

Next, there was the gentleman whose body was pulled from the ocean at East Beach. Did a passerby pull the body from the cold ocean surf, only to leave before the police arrived, not wanting to get involved, or was there something more sinister involved? Or did he take a midnight swim, knowing the morning's outcome?

Poor Charlie was beaten to death at his camp. No dignity there, just a travesty of justice, the betrayal of the precious gift of life. And the poor men—one was sixty-three years of age—whose stone-cold, lifeless bodies were found in the camps where they had laid down their heads for rest. What were their last thoughts? Were they of family and friends, of better times, when they had an actual bed to lie down on and a pillow beneath their heads? Or did they simply long for human connection, someone who cared that the stars were their ceiling and the hard dirt their bed?

I wonder about the pain of my friend "Linda" as her life slipped away at another camp on the freeway onramp. There was always sadness about her, like a whispery cloud of melancholy blue. And I question the loneliness and pain that chased her to the streets—her quiet stare of despair branding my heart and framing my memory. And "Chuck," a homeless man labeled "transient" by some, even though he had lived for decades in Santa Barbara, only to die on the freeway, losing the dance of death.

Matthew died next to his wheelchair in a park with the ocean off to one side. Only hours before, I had talked to him. He ignored my concerns, saying, "I'm okay, Ken," when I asked him how he was doing. I find myself looking around at times, listening for his voice and those words whispered in my ear. Many of us watched in sadness

74

when the coroner wheeled his broken and lifeless body away, each one of us lost in thoughts of what might lie ahead.

And of course the curse of substance abuse continues its terrible slash-and-burn assault on the streets, and the mentally ill still fall prey to their illness, abandoned.

"Mike" was a good friend. He was a man who was never at a loss for words; there was always a story on his lips that led to another story and yet another one. I had known him over twenty years, only to watch the cruel sickness rob him of his health. To his good fortune, he had the caring love of the of the hospice house in his final days. Family and friends were able to connect and hopefully heal old wounds. As did my friend "Michelle," who was able to reunite with her family with hospice's help. I'll always remember the day when she approached me and told me the cancer had returned. She always dressed so nicely in flowering dresses on her homeless journey—always giving others a helping hand. Much did she teach me about compassion and the proper dimensions of life.

And the others ... all of whom I will miss greatly. They all were not only our brothers and sisters but someone's mother and father, precious sons and daughters; children of god. You all will be missed.

There came a time, as there had in the past, when Death became personal, a dark acquaintance that took on form and substance. At times he was more real than all but my wife, children, and a few close friends. He had made his first appearance in Vietnam, but it wasn't till the unrelenting carnage by his scythe in Santa Barbara that the close and personal relationship became cemented.

Encounters with Death

Santa Barbara Independent.com, 2-19-09

Death grew bored as he hurried at his manic pace through Santa Barbara's homeless community. Not being satisfied with Ross's murder, he scattered bodies about—Montecito, Hitchcock, Milpas, State Street. But still his blood thirst propelled him onwards. A hurting man bleeds out on the way to Cottage Hospital—still not satisfied, he strikes next at the shelter, taking out a kind man in his macabre game of death. "John" was a gentle man with many close friends on the streets. His eyes bled the pain that circumstances had force-fed him. He was better than this, to end up dead without a home of his own. We are not talking multi-million dollar mansions but simply a place to lay his weary head down at night. A safe place, one to call his own, not shared by two hundred others, many fighting their own hellish battles of mental illness, physical disabilities, and sicknesses, a safer place than the streets, where he often found his only restless sleep at night; the streets, a place where murderers and haters cruise, looking for a perverted good time. A few years ago, the term troll hunting came into use to describe the sick game of finding an isolated homeless man that other men, as a group, could beat.

Looking down at John's body sprawled out on the cold shelter floor, I couldn't help but think how this man's tragic death would affect the other homeless shelter residents. It would be seen—no, felt—as a crushing blow, the likely outcome for many if they couldn't somehow manage to flee these streets. Hope is such a precious gift and an indispensable ingredient of life. It is also fragile, easily crushed when too many life events work against you.

Over the years, I saw how hope escaped John, how he began to question if he would ever leave the streets behind. He was too smart not to think that life had more to offer than this. Like many others, he questioned where his life had turned wrong—so very wrong. Where were the divides in the road that forever changed his life? He questioned aloud why some in the community hated him and the other homeless so much. What strange forces made some people fear him, a gentle and kind man if there ever was one?

Not to be outdone, Death made sure that LA added mass killings to His handiwork when gunmen entered a homeless camp and killed five. And, then for good measure, Death revisited LA to burn a defenseless homeless man to death.

The wrongs and pains of life are beyond John and the others. Cruel words can no longer hurt, and hateful stares fall upon closed eyes.

As for the rest of us, life goes on. Mike Foley told me that to do our job we have to embrace the concept of contradictions. I have always accepted this as part of my journey. Each homeless person I approach, I need to embrace as a friend, as someone with a future other than the streets, a future in a safe environment where their potential can be tended with compassion and dignity. Yet I know death lurks nearby, waiting, as likely an outcome as the other one that I strive for. He waits patiently for hopelessness to fertilize his fields in a toxic environment seeded with hateful words, thoughts, and glances.

Our words, gestures, thoughts, and deeds all weigh in the balance of fragile lives. For far too many, the struggle for a better life is over. Others await their immediate future with trepidation and fear.

The harsh sirens cut into the conversation that I was having with a client of mine at my desk in an SRO hotel (a low income hotel that took in welfare recipients—when we had them). We waited for the screams to fade; instead they stopped suddenly, close by. I looked anxiously at my pocket watch, realizing that "Jim" had missed his early morning appointment with me. I quickly packed up my things and headed for the door.

On the street, my attention was drawn to the flashing red and blue lights. I crossed the street and turned the corner. Two police officers stood, somewhat bored, by a delivery entrance. When I walked up to them, the older of the two asked me what I wanted. I identified myself and told them about my missed appointment and asked if that might have anything to do with why they were there. The second cop told me that a body had been found. Following his gaze, my eyes landed on a pair of legs sticking out of the end of a long cardboard box lying on its side.

"Would you mind looking at the body? See if you can ID it?" the older cop asked. I walked over to the cardboard box and knelt down. It was Jim. He had tied a tourniquet around his upper arm. He hadn't even had time to take the syringe out of his bicep before the hot shot had killed him. For some reason it reminded me of one of those flags they put in holes on a golf course. He looked oddly peaceful, like he was asleep, except for the color of his skin, which was chalky white. I didn't know him all that well, but I couldn't help but be moved that he would die like that. No one should die in the cardboard box that was his home.

Another time I was driving to another SRO hotel to visit a client. Pulling up behind me, sirens blasting, were paramedics. Once out of our vehicles, it became apparent pretty fast that we were all going to the same room. When we got there we found Walter spread out on the floor, dead. The two paramedics determined that he had been dead for some time. A young cop soon joined us. The room was small and extremely crowded. We all looked around, hoping to find the cause of death. I thought it only right to inform them that Walter had slipped back into his drug habit, that he was a needle user. He had picked up his drug habit while serving in Southeast Asia. A strange silence played out; eyes were awkwardly avoided. We were each alone, occupied with our own thoughts about being stuck by a needle in the age of AIDS, the potentially life-threatening hazards versus the needs of our jobs. Then, as if in a movie, came a melodic interlude: "A Slow Train's A Coming" drifted in from down the hall. The news of Walter's death became instantaneously known throughout the hotel, and someone had put the song on in tribute. Since many residents there were former drug abusers, his death struck close to the heart. Never again would I hear that song without thinking of that day.

Storyteller and the Season of Death

Storyteller newsletter, 2002
(Note: Storyteller is a childcare center for homeless children)

It's a strange thing to watch death. Death is more than just the mere absence of life; it's an active agent. Even though the paramedics work feverishly to save Mom's life (her street nickname), I sense it is all to no avail. The color of her skin is all wrong, an ashen gray that counter-indicated life. Her body and mind were too run down, her will to live too compromised, by the struggle of the streets. Of course the paramedics didn't know that; she hadn't been their friend for the last fifteen years.

It's winter, the season when Death stalks the shelters, looking for those too weak, too beaten down, too encumbered by the human condition to put up much resistance. He steals into their hearts and minds, looking for, and finding, willing followers.

As they wheel her out, I think of the little boy I just served soup. How much of this tragedy had he witnessed? How would it impact him? Then I think back over the last three weeks and recall the looks on the faces of the children when they saw someone else at the shelter die of AIDS. How had they been impacted by such a horrendous death? I look around for the boy, but he is gone, or more likely, swallowed up by the two hundred or so guests of the homeless shelter, who part to allow the gurney carrying Mom's body to the ambulance to pass.

Storyteller is more than just childcare. It is an enriched program that tries to teach and heal. It offers art, wholesome food, and good, caring teachers. But this morning it offers something more basic and humane. It offers homeless children a time-out, a secure environment away from the craziness, hopelessness, and despair of the shelters. It offers sanctuary during the dying season. And every day, I thank God for that miracle.

At times Death became bored and decided to rush his game.

Dying

Unpublished

"You've got to organize a protest—for a nude beach!"

"What?"

"Only you can do it!"

I looked down at David. His eyes had collapsed into his ashen face. His stomach protruded, and tubes ran into his body from the machines that kept him alive.

"Relative?" the doctor asked. She was young, a good-looking blonde, yet her aged eyes were drawn hard with judging, with too much sorrow witnessed.

"A friend. Also his social worker."

"We need a nude beach—you need ..." David began again.

"You need to hush so I can ask the doctor a few questions."

David looked from me to the doctor and back. He reminded me of a young child, innocence in his confused gaze, knowing something was going on that he couldn't fathom. He looked to be in his late *sixties, though he was forty-three. His body had shrunken and turned lumpy. His muscles had wasted to nothing, leaving mere stick arms and legs. His eyes were large, all but taking over his face. Death lingered in them, mocking life behind the intense gaze of the dying.*

"We lost David twice. He had a stomach infection, then pneumonia when he swallowed his own vomit."

This was getting harder to take. I had counseled David over the years that alcoholism always ended badly, with death dining on dead livers, rock-hard kidneys, and diseased pancreases. I had seen his swollen stomach, the sores that oozed and refused to heal, and the scars from gravity attacks when his equilibrium was stolen by 90-proof. As is par for the course with a practicing alcoholic, he shucked and jived his way around the issue, refusing to take my warnings seriously.

I tried hard to remember the man before this one: the shocking blue eyes electric with intelligence, the creative wit that knew no boundary. He was the court jester of the streets, mocking society when it turned harsh against those driven to homelessness. Out of a noble sense of defiance or justification, he was as adamant that people had a right to live on the streets as I was that street life was not the answer. I knew it was a dangerous place, with booze as both a numbing agent and the siren song to those wounded by life's pains.

What was never in contention between us was his heart. He always had a smile for me, a joke about the smug superiority of those who judged the homeless as less than worthy, of those who hung pretenses around their neck like so much jewelry.

"The ammonia levels build up because the liver no longer filters out the impurities in the blood."

"I know. I've had hundreds of clients suffering through end-stage liver failure." The good doctor was trying her best to be helpful by explaining the whys of his delusions. But like I said, I'd seen it all before. Besides, David wasn't a chapter in some medical textbook; he was my friend—a friend who was dying, and there wasn't a damn thing I could do about it.

I looked down into those trusting eyes that returned an unblinking, innocent stare. Once again I was moved by how nature, or God, took care of the dying. I have seen it so many times before: the feeling-

good delusions that set in to rob death of its terror; the fond memories from better times that robbed the unknown of its ability to traumatize. God or nature graced others with the comfort of spiritual blessing, the ability to not only accept the transition to the other side but also to welcome it in the end.

My thoughts drifted to "Virginia," who lay dying in a homeless shelter a little while back. She was tired of the pain of her many physical disabilities and the intense aloneness of life. She finally died in the intensive care unit. The hospital social worker told me she passed on in peace.

Virginia had returned from a nursing home in LA back to Santa Barbara. She came home to a—no, to the—homeless shelter that she remembered had offered her comfort and friendship in the past. It was a place that had anchored her existence when the chaos of the streets had threatened to overwhelm her, a place that had offered her friendship and acceptance without judgment, accepting her at face value for what she was, who she was. It's said that in the end we all come home, even if home is a homeless shelter.

David was discharged to his father to die, the father who had reached out with love to his dying son and to those of us who knew the David of old, before alcohol carved him up like so much wood.

I'm angry and at the same time deeply moved. I'm mad that the hideous monster of addiction took such a good man decades earlier than need be. I'm upset that Santa Barbara has been robbed of one of its better citizens, when we can use all the help that we can get. I'm sad about losing a good friend, with whom I have had the honor of sharing my existence with for the last thirty years, a man who was an institution on the streets and in many of our hearts.

But life is a journey that always ends the same way. Or as Ram Dass puts it, "Life is a sexually transmitted disease that is always fatal." So the circle completes. The sorrow of death is juxtaposed against its potential to heal, to bring life's journey to a close. David and Virginia both completed the circle. Both returned home.

At times Death became my alter-persona. I would be walking through Cottage Hospital, and a social worker or nurse would ask me to try and help identify a homeless man or woman who had been brought in to ICU. The last man was someone who had attempted to negotiate the freeway while intoxicated. He was all busted up and brain dead.

I can't even begin to remember all the conversations I've have with the coroner's office, staffed by caring and decent people who do all they can to identify the unknown homeless who end up in their morgue by the score every year. Or the many times a homie has stopped me in the streets to pass on the news of someone's demise, knowing, hoping, that someone besides the streets care.

Some homeless become despondent about life on the streets and in the shelters, about the unrelenting pain and isolation of their lives, and hurry death along. Sadly, others are driven to despair and depression by the hatred and harsh words directed their way by some in our community. Violence threatens those without homes on a daily basis, and murderers sometimes seek them out.

So many have killed themselves over the years that I can't remember all of them. Sometimes it's readily apparent that they view suicide as their only alternative. Other times it was not so obvious to either them or me that they viewed suicide as the answer, but, tired of the pain, they looked for a way out by ingesting vast quantities of alcohol or drugs or engaging in other extremely risky behavior. Still others couldn't face suicide on such blatant terms, so they sought death on the installment plan. However they do it, people driven by their own despair and pain, or punished by others by cruel words and deeds, will follow destructive roads that leave no doubt as to where the journey ends.

Murder by Words

Noozhawk.com, 10-08

The homeless men stood around me, rubbing sleep and the aftereffects of forty pounders, as forty ounces of beer and malt liquor are known on the street, from their eyes. To a man, they looked like a casting call for Lord of the Rings. All wore long hair and beards and the scruffy, hard look of the troubled and unforgiving lives they led. After I had exchanged the morning's pleasantries with them and made sure there were no immediate emergencies to take care of, I turned to leave, only to be stopped cold. "You need to check up on 'Captain.' He got jumped by three guys."

"Also 'Chuck,'" one of the others added. I knew Chuck was Captain's road dog—his traveling friend—a genial and good-hearted fellow veteran of the streets and of the military.

"Why Chuck?" I asked.

"He got knifed," came the casual reply.

"Was he hurt bad? Did he go to the hospital?"

No on both accounts was the response.

I turned and continued my journey down the street, my mood darker than moments before. Captain and I had a long history together. We were both Marine combat vets from Vietnam. The war had taken us down different paths upon our return—one to the streets, one to serve the streets, but in the end, the war took its pound of flesh and blood from us both.

My steps rang hollow along deserted State Street. Only the clean-up crews, the homeless, and me walked the streets that early in the morning. The city was ours alone for a brief time—time enough for me to remember something Captain had told me a few weeks back: He had been deep in sleep one night, only to be suddenly awakened when someone picked up his wheelchair and crashed it down on him. I asked if his assailant had said anything that might help identify him.

"'Bum.' He simply said 'bum.'" Captain laughed his goodhearted retort, which said he accepted such travesties of life as normal.

My mood became even darker as I thought back to the handiwork of some real heroes a few weeks before who had "tuned up" a homeless woman sleeping alone in her camp. Of course she shouldn't sleep alone in a camp. But nobody should be homeless in such a rich country as ours. Nor should a hundred-bed shelter remain empty because it's convenient for someone. And it should go without saying that he-men shouldn't go around beating up women, either housed or homeless. I remember when she stood before me, her eyes partially shut, deep purple wounds spilling from under both. She was a fragile yet hardened woman of the streets, lucky to have survived the beating—perhaps not so lucky next time.

And now death comes violently to a gentle homeless man who called Santa Barbara home. He was not a transient but a long-time resident of our community. His crime? He succumbed to life's trials and tribulations and sought refuge on the streets. Some sick individuals took prejudice to an extreme degree and beat Gregory to death in I.V., a college town just north of Santa Barbara. Of course rumors flooded the streets about who did it. I will not add to the conjectures that are adding so much fear and confusion to an already reeling and vulnerable population. I expect the police to do their job as professionals and find the sick men who kill for thrill. But I would like to remind the community where prejudicial language leads the morally weak among us.

George Orwell taught us that words have power—that they could be used to enlighten or enslave, that war can be waged as peace and enslavement couched as freedom. Bum. Transient. Fruitcase. Crazy. Drunkard. These words are used to dehumanize the homeless and/or the mentally ill, anyone who becomes a casualty of the human condition. We all should be cognizant that some among us find justification for violence behind such words. When we carelessly banter such words about, we demonize the powerless and dehumanize those who are easy prey to the darker sides of our minds.

It would do good to remember that the Buddha walked with the untouchables and broke bread with them, that Christ cast his lot with the lepers and the undesirables of his time. In fact all great religions and moral codes teach us to reach out to the less fortunate. In doing so, we honor their teachings.

There is no glory to be found in portraying the defenseless and unhoused in language that provokes our prejudices and fears, just as there was no glory in beating a gentle man to death, or jumping a Vietnam vet in the middle of the night, or "tuning up" a homeless woman. As Captain deserved a better, more welcoming home than he got, Gregory deserved our compassion and understanding, and the beaten woman should encounter love and caring rather than violence. As Orwell so elegantly wrote and wisely foresaw, language can lead to tragic consequences.

So many died. So many continue to die. I've seen enough of Death to last a lifetime, but he never tires of his job. Often when I'm driving around town, I see places where my clients' bodies—my friends—have been found. An underpass, a hotel, an empty field where a low-income hotel used to be, a bus bench, a gazebo, a park, an out-of-the-way alley, the beach … In a tourist town where the wealthy come to play and Hollywood refugees migrate, a ghost army of the deceased poor haunts its shadows. Beneath the glitter and sometimes crassness of Santa Barbara, pain collects by the ton, one lost soul at a time. Each person was somebody: someone's son or daughter, someone's mother or father. They were someone before the streets claimed them. And they were someone while they lived on those streets. Their lives and deaths shouldn't be discarded like so much trash. Santa Barbara is a city were over two hundred and fifty bodies fell in a handful of years. It is a city haunted by the spirits of the lost souls that walk lonely patrols.

Murderers Among Us

Santa Barbara Independent, Letters to the Editor, 11-6-08

Five people were shot to death in a homeless camp. Two weeks earlier a homeless man was burned to death in a vicious hate crime in the City of Angels. These stories came to us from Los Angeles, but locally, the murder of Gregory Ghan, a gentle homeless man of our community, hardly raises a stir. It's been over six months since his tragic death, and still Gregory's cowardly murderers continue to walk our streets—free men who taunt justice, mocking all who are sickened by the injustice. A wise man once said, "Justice delayed is justice denied." The denial of justice has gone on too long for Gregory. And now it appears that an open hunting season on the homeless has descended upon us. Hate crimes against the homeless, some resulting in death, has skyrocketed across the country. Even the LA Times felt compelled to run an editorial about this matter, and the News-Press ran a front-page article on these vicious attacks against the homeless. But locally, little moral outrage is expressed about Gregory's death.

Regardless of how we feel about the homeless, I think we all can agree that death handed out by cowardly hoodlums cannot be tolerated. Among the multitude of laws and infractions aimed at the homeless, nowhere is capital punishment the penalty.

Unless we citizens respond with moral outrage to these twisted crimes, I fear more of the poor and weak will pay the ultimate price for hatred and prejudice. Violence is ugly—indifference to it is so much more so. Tolerance of violence eats away at who we are as both individuals and a community.

A good start to counteracting this plague would be the apprehension and prosecution of the cowardly individuals who descended as a savage hunting pack upon Gregory. We can demand no less.

CHAPTER TEN

Something was wrong. The year 2009 rang in as death sprinted through the homeless community. I had been here before. During the age of AIDS, the crack epidemic, and the other years that spiked high death rates in our homeless community, I saw the streets suffer through it alone. In years past, such death rates were a hidden tragedy that was swept under the rug; everyone could ignore it if no one knew. In 2009, as the news of street deaths began to build, I made a pledge to myself that it would be different this time. No matter how the year played out, I would write about the deaths and the individuals behind the statistics. For once Santa Barbara citizens would not be able to say that they were unaware of the tragic deaths. This time citizens would share the pain and despair that the homeless feel when they see so many of their friends fall.

A warning is appropriate here: I am not the official note-taker for death. I do, however, keep journals of the history of the streets, and when I hear of a death, I record the person's name and something personal about them when possible. One might think that someone in an official capacity within the city or county would keep records of homeless deaths, but no one does—maybe because no one cares. At times, my journal entries may be inaccurate. I record things I hear after I verify what I can, but I'm a social worker, not an investigator. I know I also miss some deaths. I am sure that there were more deaths among our homeless friends than I recorded. But at least I tried.

My tactic of sharing this burden with the community at large met with much resistance. To some it was an embarrassment. Even some homeless advocates questioned the tactic. There were calls within the Internet community to "let the thinning begin." I guess death wasn't working fast enough for some. But I stayed true to my vow and recorded and published the reality of the deaths as I became aware of them.

If this was sometimes hard for me, it must had been doubly difficult for Bill Macfadyne, the publisher of noozhawk.com, the online news service that hosts my ongoing column. Never once did he shy away from publishing my articles, though I'm sure a lot of pressure must had been directed his way. Death in the streets is not a popular topic and not Bill's cause, but he believes firmly in the freedom of the written word, and I also feel he is a decent man, moved deeply by the pain and sorrow of those who experience life and death on our streets.

Many of the following articles in this section reflect my attempt to bring the carnage to the public's attention. They also reflect my desire to combat some hate-mongering and the all-too-frequent use of prejudicial terms against the homeless.

A Plea for Justice and Mercy

Noozhawk.com, 2-7-09

The news trickles in, slowly at first. A homeless man dies in Montecito in front of Von's. The next week, a body is found downtown on a bench. Then rumors begin to conflict with reality: A homeless man in a wheelchair was supposedly found dead; exactly when and where changes with each new report. That news sent me to the streets to check on the well-being of Freedom and Shaky Gator and Greg, plus many more. I found each of these gentlemen, except Freedom, who still remains missing. All of these wounded neighbors of ours are in varying stages of slow death. They each bear the telltale signs of years of abuse and neglect—of the toll that the hard life on the streets takes on the body and soul. Yet, regardless of their fate and pain, each wears a gentle smile and sends a warm hello in appreciation of the people who care about their well-being here in Santa Barbara. They share similar stories; they hope the slow suicide of the streets will turn out differently for them, and they share wistful plans and dreams to turn fate around. But in the end, sorrow leaks from downcast eyes, acknowledging the hideous pull the streets and death has on each of them.

With far-away looks in aged eyes sunk deep in weathered faces, they share the precious gift of warm memories of family and friends. Then come the stories of better times, followed slowly by the memories of the painful speed bumps on the road of life that sent them careening toward these cruel streets.

As for Freedom, I still am unable to track him down. I contacted my official sources, and they assured me no body of a wheelchair-bound homeless man has been found. I want to believe this, but in my extensive journey through the beaches, parks, shelters, and homeless encampments, no Freedom. The slightly built man with doleful eyes is nowhere to be found.

More bad news: the word from the streets is that "Skippy" has died from a blood infection. I talk to his girlfriend, who confirms the news of this latest tragedy through her tears. Next the kind folks from Holy Chaos call me. On their way to the YMCA, they stumble upon paramedics trying to revive a homeless man found down on the sidewalk. Sadly, it was to no avail. Jack and Ruth, the kind people who run this faith-based outreach to the homeless, are deeply saddened by this news. While sharing their loss, they remind me of the good people in our community who find love in their hearts and reach out to the less fortunate. Jack and Ruth are not professionals, nor have they been at this very long—not long enough to have experienced the deaths of hundreds of homeless men and women and one small baby, as I have during my professional career on our streets. But with their kind hearts and caring ways, they help ground me; they help me hold onto the belief that together, as a community, the housed and unhoused can come together to end this slow-motion horror show. With compassion, we can say, "Enough excuses"—enough turning our backs on the mentally ill, the newly jobless, the physical disabled, the veterans of the endless wars, and a whole lot of people who are just down on their luck or casualties of hard economic times that they had nothing to do with. If anything, the massive layoffs and the cruelty of our broken medical and mental health delivery systems should allow us to recognize our fellow citizens without judgment and condemnation. The newly homeless and the chronic are not given the multi-million dollar golden parachute for excessive greed that now rains down so much pain upon millions of Americans. No, no golden parachutes, winks, nor false handshakes are to be theirs. Instead, a cold night on the beach, a frightful night in an alley or park awaits them for a few troubled hours.

In the meantime, I continue my search for Freedom, to either confirm or lay to rest one more story of a cold and lonely death on our streets. Without him, 2009 starts out with four deaths among our homeless friends; with him, there are five—a cold way to start a new year.

Postscript

This week two more homeless men died. "Charlie" lived the last of his existence at the shelter, slowly losing the battle against his debilitating disease, along with his will to live. More tragically, Ross, a man who battled both mental and physical disabilities, was cruelly beaten to death last night on East Beach. It's been eight months now, and still the police have not made an arrest in the Gregory Gahn case. The word filters down to me to be patient. How long should one wait for justice? And now, again, murder strikes the homeless. Enough is enough. Gregory awaits justice. Anywhere else, these are called hate crimes but not here. Instead, cruel "opinion" pieces in some news medias mask the contempt that some have towards the homeless.

A Rush to Judgment

Noozhawk.com, 3-20-09

I learned, with shock and dismay, that the police closed the murder investigation into the Ross Stiles' murder yesterday, after barely five weeks. His murderers will go scot-free for this heinous crime. Confusion and sadness followed when other information came to my attention. First, Ross suffered from a "massive swelling of the brain." He had reported to his friends that he had been assaulted days before he was admitted to the hospital with a severe headache. Eyewitnesses reported seeing two men fleeing his camp after hearing glass break. And then I learned that the police have closed their case, while the coroner's case is still open. And the questionable press release that seemed to go out of its way to report that Ross was drunk at the time he was admitted to the hospital begs the question. Does this serve any purpose other than to color the story and put Ross in a negative light? And where did the reported blood alcohol content, or BOC, come from? It is my understanding that the toxicology report has not yet been completed.

The next day, a man whom Ross had told about the assault told me the police hadn't interviewed him since the day before Ross died. Another man who shared the campsite and was present at the time of the assault also told me he hadn't been interviewed since the first day of the investigation. In fact, I have talked to no one who has been interviewed in the last few weeks.

This kind of violence can never be tolerated. Ross was a gentle man, crippled with severe pain in his hips and legs and battered by personal demons. It must have taken a couple of real men to come into his camp and assault him like that—cowards come to mind. I know some will say he shouldn't have been sleeping outside. Without engaging in the debate about where the fault lies, homelessness is not a capital offense. Ross did not deserve to die like that—nobody does. Even at the bedrock of our society, justice must be equal for all, rich and poor alike. Both sides of the homeless debate should unite as one and demand justice for Ross. Everyone must denounce violence, which in the end debases us all. As citizens of a democratic society, we have the right, and at times the moral obligation, to petition our government to right such a wrong. We should respectfully contact the police and asked that the case be reopened, witnesses reexamined, and everything possible be done to bring his murderers to justice. When we do so, we need to show the police the respect that we ask them to show Ross. We will not turn to hateful nor harsh rhetoric but simply ask that they join us in bringing a measure of justice to a disenfranchised community.

Faces

Noozhawk.com, 3-31-09

The new year roared in on a deadly wind. With this strong gale at his back, Death was in a frantic race toward a macabre finish line. He sprinted through the homeless community as if he were behind with some cruel quota. Eleven people who had found the street to be their home away from home have succumbed to his deadly charms. His choice of weapons was as broad as they were ruthlessly mundane. He found his work to be easy. The victims, all long-time homeless with deep roots in that community, were weakened by years on the streets and in homeless shelters. Hunger exhausted their bodies. Shattered self-esteem lowered the natural defenses of mind and body. Stress of an unimaginable quality gorged on them as it tore at vital organs. Some had turned to the numbing relief of alcohol, an attempt at self-medicating that damaged livers and ate away the will to live. Exposure to the elements also had a hand. Imagine sitting in a rainstorm or sleeping in winter rains, being awakened by bone-shattering shivers—a cold so intense that it threatened to shred muscles to ribbons.

Sadly, a considerable number of the homeless are the vulnerable mentally ill. And increasingly, many homeless are the long-term physically disabled who lack the financial means to medically fight their conditions; increasingly the frail elderly and women have been turned out to the streets.

A problem, one of many with this scale of death, is the inability to process and grieve the recently departed—to show them proper respect. An example: when I first heard of Ross's murder, I was talking to someone about the death of a veteran who had gone to a Los Angeles medical facility to fight and then die of an infection. Someone came up and interrupted to notify me that Ross had been murdered. This news was unreal and hard to take, as I had talked to Ross just the week before. I questioned the deliverer of the bad news, thinking he had misheard my conversation: was he talking about the vet we had been talking about? "No," he replied. "Ross."

The next day I hit the camps and beaches, looking for answers about this cowardly crime. It must have taken a great amount of courage for two men to beat a nearly crippled man to death. But suddenly the tragic death of "David" fought for attention. I remember his sad, downcast eyes as, over the years, he fought his losing fight with diabetes. It is a disease that many Americans fight successfully, but such a contest in a homeless shelter involves cruel odds. I can still see him; the hard knowledge that his last months on earth would *be in a shelter shattered his will to live. But before I could properly honor his passing, I find myself upstairs at the shelter, looking down on the dead body of "Doug." On the floor at my feet, his unfocused eyes stared back at me. I knew Doug well. He was a man hounded by physical disabilities that pounded depression down his throat. He was a gentle man, with many friends in the shelter and the streets. Walking away from his body and down the stairs, I cringed, knowing how those who knew him would take the news. In the lobby, pain was etched on many faces.*

Fighting to maintain control in the face of all the recent deaths, I started to approach the streets with caution. I needed time; we all needed a break from Death's presence. But it was not to be. Like a bomb going off, the news came that Chris had died. An image of her soft face framed by brown hair came easily. Her cautious eyes were also sorrowful—which is the way I would describe the others in this article. Something about living on the streets reveals the frailty of life and its harshness—a knowledge that cripples many and ushers Death in. Immediately, I began to ask around about Max, her German shepherd. I've owned shepherds all my adult life, and it was a magical connection between Chris and myself. We often passed the time talking about them. I think she did so as a means of escape, of pushing the violence that had shoved her to the streets into the background. I guess she no longer needs this.

But before I could track Max down, still more devastating news came of two more homeless deaths; two citizens tried to keep warm by bringing a generator into their RV. They died peacefully in their sleep. But why? They knew about the dangers and in fact had never brought the generator inside before. They always ran it outside the rig. Why this time? Why?

I approach my friends on the streets and in the shelters gingerly now, looking into their eyes to see if liquid pain is to be found there. I exhale gratefully when I see only the run-of-the-mill sadness of the homeless, not another death notice. Just the "run-of-the-mill sadness of the homeless." How sad that it has all come down to this.

Update

    While writing this article, I was informed that "George" died of heart failure. This elderly man's death is the twelfth since January 1. And since the original update, another homeless person died. "Sherry" was a good friend of mine for years. This latest news is a crushing blow, but her story deserves an article of its own. It feels like I'm standing on the train tracks, death an onrushing train.

The Miracle Jacket

Noozhawk.com, 4-8-09

    "Sherry," you should know that it was Jerry who told me of your death. He was just this side of a seizure that threatened to topple him over. I quickly sat him down. The odor of stale beer hung heavily in the small office. His rheumy eyes were sadder than usual. He took the news of your death very personally, realizing that his future was there.

    I sat there, speechless, looking for an alternative explanation. You see, your boyfriend came to me just last week, saying he was concerned about you, telling me how weak you were. I told him to take you to the hospital. He was reluctant and said he had taken you twice already and they had refused treatment and, in fact, threatened to have you arrested for public intoxication. Knowing such stories are often exaggerations, though sometimes true, and also knowing there was no alternative, I quickly came up with a battle plan. If he would go back to camp and call 911, I would arrange for a bed for you at the shelter if and when the hospital should cut you loose. My hoped-for plan was to have you hospitalized and stabilized before you were placed at the shelter to work with Larry, a great recovery coach with a ton of contacts in the sober community. The best laid plans of mice and men ...

    Jerry was scared. His shoulders pinched painfully together with the knowledge that he wasn't far behind you. He was so weak that I had to help him stand. He had been hospitalized twice recently, once with pneumonia, and had also been beaten by kids out for a thrill. He agreed to go over to Project Recovery and check himself into detox. After he left, I hit the streets, looking for the answers to his tragic news so I could somehow understand your death—the one death of a friend, someone who was not simply a cold statistic to me.

I found them, your friends and boyfriend, huddled together as if trying to give each other comfort—or perhaps they were circling the wagons for protection from predatory death. They were quiet when I approached, and we welcomed each other with downcast eyes. Perhaps we were all shielding our souls from survivor's guilt. Your boyfriend was struggling to put your death into some kind of perspective. He told me you were in a better place now, somewhere where the pain would no longer eat your soul away a little at a time. We shared the horrendous depths where the immeasurable pain had taken each of us. We then retreated to our individual private worlds to replay our last and fondest memories of you, away from prying eyes.

I see you as you were, a beautiful Native American woman with midnight-black hair. You always had a kind word and a loud laugh for me, but behind your smile your eyes were dark with sadness. I often wondered where the fine lines of hurt that circled both your eyes came from. Maybe you had a premonition of how things would turn out. Or maybe something from your past chased you into the present. I know that when Dr. J. and I would ask you how you were doing, you always said, "Fine," which we both knew was a lie. The streets are buried under not only a sea of lies but also an ocean of falsehoods. I look back fondly now to the times when you and I would walk the cold early morning streets in our attempt to find the bridge that would enable us to reach one other beyond all the craziness, to somehow connect.

I will always remember you as you were at Christmas. A kind donation from a Santa Barbara saint allowed me to buy scores of winter jackets. Included were a few with faux fur collars. They were of a cheaper quality than the others, but you immediately asked for one of them rather than the warmer, rainproof ones. For weeks after that I never saw you without it on. You looked and acted like a little girl with a new red bicycle. I was glad to see your innocent joy come to the forefront. You had a beautiful soul, Sherry, and I hope your boyfriend was right. I hope you are in a better place, one free from the pain that tore at your soul. I miss you. We all miss you, and we are all so sorry how your life's journey turned out. Our world is a little grayer, a little colder, without you in it.

Morgue Pictures Never Lie

Noozhawk.com, 4-30-09

Morgue pictures never do justice. But they do remain with you, even after the passage of time. The phone call informed me that you were over six feet tall. I'll take their word on that. On a morgue slab, everyone is equal. Tall and short, all look the same. It's easy to see how skinny you had become in the last days of your life. If you weighed the one hundred and thirty pounds that they claimed, it was with a generous scale. Minus your false teeth, your mouth had caved in. And the eyes, your eyes, were the eyes of the dead, filmed over with a milky substance, like bad cataracts, where the sparkle of life used to shine.

The coroner is a good man. Nobody had to tell him how wrong it is for someone to die without a name. Somewhere, a brother or sister, a spouse, or, most tragic of all, children will slowly begin to dread quiet holidays even more when the silence shouts. That's why he sent me the picture, hoping against hope that I would know you.

I looked harder at the glossy photo. I recognized you in a vague way. Mid-State Street popped into my mind. It is an area of town where the mentally ill live, hide, feed, exist, a segregated community where the street culture dictates that the mentally ill street dwellers are known only by street names, if any: Red, Bushman, and Wingnut Vet. It's a closed, fragile culture, where, except by a social worker or cop, questions are not asked and answers not readily provided, and if they are, as often as not they are fabricated: a place where the misrules of delusions and paranoia run rampant.

The picture jogged my memory. Closing my eyes, I see you, Louis, with your shoulders hunched over, robbing two inches from your six-foot-four frame. I remember that your long gray hair was shot through with rivers of pure white, your chin covered with a perpetual growth of whispery whiskers. Your clothes were always dirty; while you were able to spend some time indoors at the shelter, bathing was much more problematic.

Louis, your hands were always busy. They played, insistent, maniacal, compulsive, with a deck of worn cards. Getting any information from you was next to impossible. The cards did all your talking, and they weren't saying much most of the time. They simply marked the passage of time. They hid you from the loony, lonely reality that surrounded your existence. I know that your mind had constructed a fortress that allowed few details of your sixty-some-odd years of life to leak out. You were always much better at evasiveness than I was at mining information.

I last saw you alive in a hospital bed. An ugly contusion on your forehead surprised you when I asked how you had gotten it. You didn't have the faintest idea. The hospital told me they were making arrangements to discharge you back to the shelters. I didn't see how.

The next day the call came; you had passed away in the night. I felt bad. Somewhere, someone would not know—only with time and the passage of unacknowledged holidays would the realization sink in that you were not coming back.

I once went to a symposium on end-of-life care given by good people with a good message: use the end-of-life passage as a healing process. Bring to a close any antagonistic family issues; look into your soul and connect with your belief system. Welcome the transition to the hereafter. But somehow none of that related to my clients, or to the streets.

A friend of mine put it into perspective. The homeless, in particular the mentally ill homeless, approach death as they lived their life: with chaos all around, they define who they are and what they are. How do you make a gentle transition to death when your name, the key to your identity, is locked deep behind closed lips? How do you resolve family issues when you have told others that your children and spouse are dead when they are not? How do you access quality care in the end if you lay dying in a homeless shelter, your body fluids washing the floor as your life leaks out, along with your meager hope or when medical care is delivered by an ER or a nurse who works with the homeless?

Once I tried for placement in a hospice facility for Vickie, a woman dying at a shelter, but I was told I needed a doctor's certificate to verify what I saw, what I knew. I have seen death more times than I can remember anymore. His presence has grown comfortable in a way, like a blister that refuses to heal. I see it in skin color turned bad; in eyes turning yellow then dull; in the sunken cheeks and extended livers and stomachs. I don't need verification from the medical profession, for Death waits for no man or woman; he has his own schedule, his own agenda. Vickie, you were on his to-do list.

My friend John asked, "Who cares for these people? Whose job is it to help the poorest of the poor, those in most need of housing, medical care, of love? The modern-day outcasts, the lepers of our time?"

Some cities have a pauper's cemetery, where those who have fallen off the grid of modern life end up; a place where those who escape or are condemned to live the life of the forgotten homeless finally find a home. It's a foreboding place. Those who have lost the race are buried alone, young and old, black, white, and brown, united by the fact that they left this life in isolation. They left loved ones a mystery, never to know their final outcome—brothers and sisters, husbands and wives, children with holes in their hearts and an ache in their souls, never knowing. Chaos rules.

I will always remember you, Louis, with fond memories, and the image of my friend in the morgue shot will stay with me. As for Vickie, I will always see you as a woman who died in a homeless shelter surrounded by isolation, by an aloneness that quietly engulfed you in your last moments on earth.

A Community in Pain

Noozhawk.com, 5-1-09

"Pete:" one should be careful about reading e-mails on a Sunday evening. That's how I found out about you being on life support. No other information was available; the message was brutally short. It wasn't till I hit the streets and shelters Monday morning that I heard what had happened. It was hard thinking of you strapped down to a bed in the ICU, with tubes running in and out of your body like a science project run amok, your lanky frame bundled in hospital-white sheets.

I remember talking to you just last week, helping you with forms—the bane of your existence. You had come to us from the streets, one of the lucky ones. You always had a devilish laugh for me, yet fear defined your eyes. Being on crutches on the streets must have been particularly threatening—you were a victim for any predator out there. Sorrow seemed to grow darker the longer you were in the shelter. I have seen that reaction in many long-term homeless. While on the streets, the day-to-day struggle for existence takes all your energy: where to find something to eat, where to sleep, where to be safe from the muggers that hang around Santa Barbara like a black cloud. When finally those bare necessities, and safety, are taken care of in a shelter, one's defenses naturally become lowered. You have the time and inclination to see just how far you have fallen, to face the demons that have chased you for so many years.

In your case, Pete, it was that horrible accident that brutally mutilated your leg so severely that the doctors had to cut it off. I believe the term the medical people use is traumatic amputation. I remember the first time I met you. You had trouble dragging the practically useless prosthetic leg behind you. Whoever gave it to you had done a poor job fitting it, because you were always in constant pain. And after only a few years use it was already badly damaged. It creaked loudly that day, much like the Tin Man in the Wizard of Oz when he needed oiling. Rather than helping you walk, it hindered you as you dragged it behind you.

I remember sitting across the lobby of the shelter, watching you. You looked both lost and scared. Then I remember how you told me of the trauma of the accident—of being hit by that car while you were walking: the pain and confusion, the surgery—the shock of waking up without a leg. But I also remember a kinder memory, one that produced bouts of laughter for you and me.

I was at the front desk of the shelter when a conscientious citizen came in looking for me. He stated he was glad that I was there, as he had just seen a homeless man in the ivy in the underpass on Milpas. The man had a compound-fractured leg, the lower part of it sticking out at a ninety-degree angle. I grabbed Nurse Jan Fadden and yelled at the staff to call it in. She and I ran to the underpass. Sure enough, you were in the ivy, and, sure enough, your artificial leg had finally completely broken. It was in fact sticking out at that crazy angle. The well-meaning Samaritan didn't know, of course, that it was an artificial limb. After admonishing you for scaring the hell out of Jan and I, we returned to the shelter, retrieved a wheelchair, and returned to get you. The shelter was kind enough to give us a medical bed for you.

I can still see Jan and me that day, bent over in laughter, you with that infectious chuckle rolling in the ivy. I am sure that more than one passing motorist thought Jan and I were crazy and/or cruel, laughing at a down-and-out, injured homeless man sprawled out in the ivy. For her and me, it was a way of releasing the charging adrenaline and expressing our thankfulness that human flesh hadn't been traumatized. For you, it must have been the sight of us running down the street in great haste, with looks of concern cutting into our faces. You got your revenge when I had to push the suddenly uncooperative wheelchair all the way back to the shelter. You and I continued the therapeutic laughter, trading gentle insults and stupid jokes all the way, Jan thinking that we were both crazy. But that's the way men bond and show their concern and friendship for one another, using jokes and kindly insults as the great equalizer.

But now the jokes are done with, and we grieve your passing. I will try to hold onto the lighthearted memories of that day rather than the sorrow that colored the last few weeks over the cruel turn that your life took and your untimely death. Know that your kind and infectious laughter will be missed.

Postsript

I ran the nature of your injuries past a professional. He has read literally thousands of autopsies, and he stated that it is highly improbable that those injuries could result from anything other than the hands of another. I asked him to call the coroner and request an autopsy. If your injuries were at the hands of others, then our pain is compounded by yet another murder. Hopefully a thorough police investigation and an autopsy can lay my fears to rest and lead to justice.

While on my rounds this morning, I learned of a homeless man who is in a deep coma at the Torrance Burn Center, with burns covering 60 percent of his body. While true that the man was deeply saddened by the latest deaths on the streets, it looks like he was set on fire. If so, this is a hate crime that cannot be allowed to go unpunished. It should also call for deep soul searching by all of us. The homeless community needs our help and moral support during these deeply troubled and painful times.

Less than Some

Noozhawk.com, 5-13-09

    I'm the first one to acknowledge there's much I don't know, and I understand even less. I am frequently tormented by doubt, torn by my inability to see life as it always is. I try not to jump to conclusions but also not to miss the forest for the trees. Yet, with so much death and violence impacting the homeless at this time, I feel like a drunk staggering down the street, fighting for equilibrium. Recently, when the homeless, and sometimes the cops, relate the newest atrocities of the streets, I'm unsure if I'm hearing the news right or if I should instead be questioning my sanity. I remember when I first heard of Ross's murder, I searched frantically within my brain for another angle on the story. Perhaps he fell; perhaps he succumbed to the diseases that attacked his body. But I talked to people who saw things, knew things. And then I thought back to another unsolved murder, and reality slammed me into dark corners where I'd rather not be.

    Recently, while working my rounds of the camps and streets, I was informed that Alan, a wheelchair-bound man, was at Cottage Hospital on life-support. This was the same man that I had received an e-mail about, telling me the same story. But a new twist was added. He had wounds, usually caused at the hands of another. While trying to process this information, I ran into a homeless woman who told me of another homeless man, Alex, who had been set on fire. I was again staggered, trapped in a cloud of confusion by this newest onslaught against human decency. I checked her story about Alex with other professionals, and they confirmed at least part of it. A homeless man was in fact lying in a coma, with burns covering 60 percent of his body, but he couldn't tell the authorities much because his injuries were so severe and life-threatening.

Walking the streets more slowly now, I tried to make sense of it all. The first thing I feared was a rush to judgment (I've been there before) and that Alan, who succumbed to his wounds, would be cremated before an autopsy could be performed. Did I know for sure how he died? Obviously not. But I did know that without the findings of the coroner, the answers would be lost forever. I contacted my attorney friend, Joe Allan, and asked him to request that an autopsy be performed. He was kind enough to do so.

Again, while working my rounds, Lynne Janhke, MD, and I heard more troubling news. Within a day, I found out that six other homeless persons had been assaulted. As far as I could tell, at least four of them appeared to be gang violence: a group of young men were going around beating the homeless. For what? Kicks? Gang initiation? Or simple stupidity force-fed by testosterone? The only thing for sure that morning was that I stood on Haley St. looking into a young, boyish face with stitches running over one eye and looping downwards. Another man stood by, telling me a similar story while holding his broken hand gingerly. Suddenly Alan and Alex's injuries were put in a context that added a terrifying dimension. I fear what the connected dots meant.

I, of course, am neither cop nor coroner. I rely on their expertise and sense of honor and ethics to answer these troubling questions. The only thing I know for sure is that I now walk in fear along with the homeless; they fear bodily injury and death, and I dread the next story and what the next encounter with a homeless person might divulge. I wait, ever more anxious and despondent, for all this madness to subside, while paranoia battles reality. I wasn't particularly good at running from the truth in Vietnam. Violence changes us, with its dehumanizing effects. I guess I haven't changed all that much.

Updates

The murder case of Ross Stiles, which had been closed by the police, has quietly been reopened. Why? What has changed? What new evidence or witnesses have come forward? As for the Gregory Ghan case, we approach the one-year anniversary of his death, his murderers still running free. And Alex continues his existence in a coma, suffering the hell of a burn victim. All these cases cry out for justice.

This next article reflects my attempt to bring the healing powers of the community as a whole to the homeless during such trying times. I also hoped that with the publicity, the powers-that-be would be forced to step forward and do something to stop the carnage. Unfortunately, the high death rate continued for the rest of the year and into the beginning of the next.

Homeless Memorial: A Gesture of Grace

Noozhawk.com, 7-6-09

So many homeless people have died this year, it's hard to remember them all—that is, till I walk the streets and sense their absences. Though some may not care, the essence of our community has changed. Many of the homeless who died had talents and caring souls; they did what they could to help those in even worse shape than themselves. And, as in any group of people, the homeless who died run the gauntlet of types of personalities. While some had gruff exteriors, hardened by the unforgiving streets over the years, others were highly sensitive and deeply wounded by the harsh judgments and mean-spirited words others directed their way.

Since those individuals without homes were taken by Death, it was all but impossible to honor their individual passing. Their deaths came too fast and unrelenting. To help rectify this, a pair of memorials will be held, in conjunction with the Greater Santa Barbara Clergy Association. It is our hope that the memorials will remind us all of the fragility, as well as the sanctity, of life. The first memorial service is scheduled for July 13, 2009, at 2:30 PM. It will be held next to the East Beach public bathroom, across the street from the Red Lion Inn—the location where Ross Stiles was murdered. It will be held there to keep us all focused on the violent death of this man and to remind us that his and Gregory Ghan's murderers still roam free. This first service is particularly for the homeless and those who serve them, day in and day out. But it is open to any member of our city who wishes to show respect and share the loss of our homeless friends who have died.

So far this year, seventeen homeless people have died. Here are their stories.

Chris and Stephanie were perhaps the deepest losses, the ones that hurt the most. When I think of Chris I cannot help but think of her dog Max, her gentle and always faithful German shepherd, her constant companion. Whenever Chris was in the shelter, Max was never far from her side. To think of her dying away from her best friend was a particularly bitter insult. Max was always there as her protection. He was Chris's attempt to deal with the violence that had chased her to the streets in the first place. As for Stephanie, she was a warm woman who added brightness to the most dreary of street mornings. Unfortunately, the pain that colored her eyes such a deep brown never left her for a moment. She was a good friend and is missed by many.

Ross Stiles' death was particularly shocking; an infirmed, disabled man was killed over a sleeping bag. That life can be reduced to the price of a used sleeping bag is unfathomable.

As for Joe, it was hard to witness his gradual collapse, first his body then his will to live, over the prolonged time he spent with us at the shelter. He was a man condemned to his wheelchair and haunted by an unbending system that he just never seemed to fit within.

The death of military veterans is always poignant. We pay special honor to Robert and "Michael."

Alan's death was difficult to handle. He fought daily against his depression from the accident that crippled him. The unanswered questions as to the true nature of his death adds a somber note to his memory for me. I will always see the sadness that defined this man's existence while he questioned how his life had gone so terribly wrong.

Sometimes the death of an elder is as surreal as the death of a child. Perhaps it was Gayle's advanced age that set him apart, but his passing sent ripples of sadness through the providers at the shelter. Maybe it was because he was so terribly alone when he became ill and then died, without friends or family at his side.

Damon had a host of friends who cared deeply for him. His youth made him the youngest and arguably the best liked of those who have passed away since January 1st, 2009. I will always remember his conflicted look when he told us the bizarre story of how a citizen had unwrapped his ace-bandaged foot and then walked away. Had the person simply forgotten him or become distracted? It was a small mystery that in many ways defines the surreal world of the streets. It is a story that I will always think about when I remember Damon.

The sudden deaths of EZ and Anita came at a particularly low time on the streets. They followed Ross's murder, and the weird nature of their deaths cut deeply. Jeremy died at the shelter and Ron on the beach. Perhaps the cruelest deaths are those of the unknown. First, there was a man who died in Montecito; then an unknown body was found at Milpas Street, and a man died across the street from the YMCA.

I am deeply grateful to and would like to thank those who make this noble gesture possible, in particular Rev. Teena Grant, Cottage Hospital chaplain, who helped give birth to this idea; the Greater Santa Barbara Clergy Association; Don Johnson of the Montecito Covenant Church; the Community Kitchen; Casa Esperanza; Larry Jewel; and John Buttny of the Ten Year Plan to End Chronic Homelessness. And most importantly, Morris Bear, a world-renowned artist who has agreed to create a sculpture to honor our deceased friends. These people show us all by their example that spiritual values are not simply to be preached and listened to once a week but to be lived daily. They remind us that, regardless of our positions in life, we all possess a soul, and that a community is all-inclusive, running the gauntlet from the richest to the poorest. We are all less for the untimely passing of our homeless friends. I deeply miss them all.

A Lonely Death, a Father's Prayer

Noozhawk.com, 9-9-09

How does one die alone in modern society, in our bustling city? How does one pass over to the other side with no one noticing that you are no longer around? Did he have no loved one or simple friend who missed him when he failed to show up for the small graces of life that we all take for granted? Were all his meals eaten alone? Did he not even partake in the ancient ritual of breaking bread with others? Did he receive no mail, no correspondence, that connected him with family elsewhere?

Redbeard's cold and lifeless body was hidden by uncounted time, much like his existence—the person he was, was concealed behind his mental illness. Did he die with the sounds of manic rush hour traffic in his ears, like soothing hypnotic music? Or perhaps the quieter sounds of lonely cars swishing by in the dead of night, smothered by all that darkness.

Did Redbeard become suddenly ill, or had he simply grown weary? Did he decide to lay his head down for some rest behind the bushes on 101, never to open his eyes again? Or did he know that he was dying?

What was Redbeard's real name? Were a mother and father left wondering what had happened to their mentally ill son? Or perhaps a wife was left to fathom the cruel twists and turns of life without her partner, her soulmate. Or did he leave behind a child, alone and adrift, without a father to fathom the cruel realities of mental illness, left to speculate about how it drove his dad away from his loved ones?

Maybe in the end Redbeard's life simply became too much—too much pain, too much aloneness—and then, and only then, did the darkness beckon.

Redbeard was like many of the mentally ill homeless I have known. Their backgrounds are lost to a torrent of delusional hallucinations so profound and so deep that they altered their reality, thus changing their personal history. The present, filled with pain, aloneness, and fright, is all that exists for them. This present is without four walls or structures of any kind, a cruel world without cause and effect, ruled too often by demons of the mind and caprice. It is a world without logic; how else can one explain that a mentally ill wounded person living in the richest city in the richest country in history should die alone and penniless alongside a freeway, just miles away from multi-million-dollar mansions. He existed in a living hell, where most, if not all, others were perceived as threats, as vengeful gods hurling insults, insinuations, and accusations.

Mental illness is so terrifying because you are so all alone. It is a disease that mandates all too often that you suffer by yourself, without anyone to share the burden of that particular pain. You wake up alone, eat alone, live your existence alone, and frequently die alone, as did Redbeard. There's no one to tell you that the terror of the nightmares aren't real—just the opposite: they are everything.

Redbeard passed quietly, missed by some in the community who no longer saw the presumed veteran walking our streets stoutly with his head held high. He was the twenty-first homeless person out of twenty-three to die this year, a year that becomes increasingly bitter as time and the body count mounts.

Thinking of Redbeard's life journey, I wondered about his trajectory from his teen years to the descent into mental illness. At work I keep half a picture of a young woman on her eighteenth birthday—it's only half, as her father had torn it so that the rest of the family was not included. He had come to Santa Barbara years ago following his runaway daughter's tracks. She had dropped the family a postcard from our community after her escape from Silicon Valley. I remember him as a wealthy, well-dressed, important man who had ditched his tie in respect when visiting me to ask my help.

His story was familiar to me—way too familiar—but its commonality didn't dampen the pain that flowed from this man's broken heart. I couldn't help but think as he sat across from me that he was my mirror opposite, except in one dimension: He, like me, was a father, and the love of our children we shared exposed us to a hellacious pain all its own, as any parent can attest to. He went on to explain that his daughter had suffered her first psychotic break soon after the picture was taken. I remember looking closer at the picture in my hand and seeing the gathering darkness in the young woman's eyes. Already the terror of mental illness was to be found there.

Giving me his business card, he asked me to call him if contact was made. He lost the battle with his cool business persona and let his father's pain plead for my help. Of course, I told him I would try. I withheld the knowledge of just how daunting it would be to find a mentally ill girl in the open-air asylum that our city streets had become.

I slip the picture back into my drawer and pray that the man finally found his daughter—alive. That she received help and was able to beat the disease and put the streets behind her. Redbeard's parents will never have that prayer fulfilled.

All year long Death continued his macabre collection of souls. Many caring citizens in Santa Barbara were moved by the deaths among our neighbors on the streets. For others, it was merely an excuse to continue their hateful campaign against the homeless.

To the friends no longer with us …

In Memory of Those Who Died in 2009

Noozhawk.com, 12-21-2009

I am one of those people who still likes this time of year. While it's true that the commercialism leaves me cold, I have made a commitment not to let the desire of some to make a fast buck ruin what should be a time of spiritual reflection for all of us; and, I am proud to say that many in our community do just that. Be they Christian, Jew, Muslim, or non-believer, many people take this time for such soul searching, and they act upon those spiritual beliefs. This is also the time of year that I stop and pay homage to those who have passed on. Obviously, since I work with the homeless, my thoughts turn to those on the streets who have died. I have one bit of good news to report in this regard. Michael B., who I last had a conversation with at Project Healthy Neighbors that led me to believe that he had stumbled and became homeless again, was in fact on the road to recovery and was housed. He was known and loved by many, and his passing touched us all.

Chris and I shared a special relationship built around our love of German shepherds. (I hope my new puppy, an English mastiff, understands about this.) Her dog, Max, was a companion dog. Everyone at the shelter that temporarily became their home loved him. After Chris's brutal attack, which left her impaired and drove her to the streets, it was Max she turned to for support. He was also her protector when she was forced to flee to the often-brutal streets. During our shared stories of our dogs, the sadness and pain would momentarily lift from her eyes. She could forget for at least a little while that at one time she had been a different woman, one who owned a small business. I wonder if the men who so viciously attacked her are proud of what they turned her into?

The cold weather with frost on the roofs reminds me of "Sherry." The early mornings on lower State St. belong to the workers keeping our city clean, the cops, the homeless, and me. During those reflective times, Sherry and I would often walk together. Her eyes were chiseled hard, hiding the pain that lapped at her soul. I was never able to discover the source of her pain. One morning, I had two winter coats: one was weatherproof, the other a lighter one, with a fake fur collar. Thinking she would prefer the heavier one to ward off the cold, I offered it to her. While thanking me, her eyes kept drifting back to the lighter one. When I offered her that one instead, a youthful sparkle brightened up her eyes. For the few months remaining of her life, I never saw her again when she wasn't wearing that coat.

I never did find out the source of the infection that killed Robert. Like me, he had served in the military. We frequently shared our vet stories. I miss him.

I witnessed sadly the slow progression of Joe's disease, which ate away savagely at his body. His spirit was destroyed a little at a time, till the wheelchair that enslaved became his casket.

I would often visit Ross Stiles at his campsites, trying to encourage him to come into the shelters or to at least allow the medical staff to treat his crippling disabilities. During those visits, I found myself squatting down so I wouldn't tower over him. The pain that twisted his body prevented him from standing. I will remember till the day I die sitting at a homeless shelter reading a vicious anti-homeless article that a man who called the streets home had given me. He had been deeply hurt by the tone of the piece. I remember trying to downplay it—saying that was merely one person's opinion. The next person in line came to give me bad news. He knew that I was close to Ross and wanted me to know of his death. I sat in shock at first, not believing what I was being told. To this day, the murder of the crippled, gentle man has gone unsolved.

And it is still a mystery to me how EZ and Juanita died from carbon monoxide poisoning. They had lived on the streets long enough to know not to run a generator within the tight confines of a rig. Did the cold drive them to such a fatal decision, or was something else at play?

To this day, I am still not convinced that Alan died the way they said he did. How can an amputee who is restricted to a wheelchair fall hard enough forward to die from a blow to the head? I also understand that he had two head wounds. Facts are hard to come by on the streets—the only certainty is this man's tragic death.

I can still see the body of Jeremy lying at my feet. He had passed away at a shelter, and we were waiting for the coroner. He seemed peaceful—his struggle was finally over. The same can be said of Mitch, though the day before he died, he told several people that he felt the presence of death lurking about.

There are those who died without names, and still others too numerous to detail: Guitar Man, Redbeard, John, Gayle and Ron, Robert, and Damon and Tom, a gifted artist whose talents will now never be acknowledged. May they all pass into a more peaceful hereafter. May we, as a community, stop for a moment and give a simply prayer or take a moment to reflect. May those who feel so moved renew our dedication to the fight to return the social plight of homelessness back to the history books, where it belongs. May the soup kitchens and shelters be once again found only in the history of the Great Depression and not in our communities.

And let the families of the men and women who fell in Afghanistan and Iraq find peace of mind during these sure to be trying holidays—and may no more fall. Finally, may our deepest values, which hold life sacred, see the light of day.

A Sad Update

After finishing this article, I was informed that Freedom died during the freezing cold, sitting in his wheelchair on State Street. He had told many that this was to be his last year on the streets: He had heard Death's approaching footsteps. I was surprised how many knew this homeless vet and how many were touched by his infectious humor. Thank you to all who had kind words regarding this man and took the time to share them. I'm sure it meant a lot to him.

Like a Broken Doll

Excerpt from: For the Love of Death

"Who are you?" William Derek asked, ignoring the attempt of his coworker Hammond to warn him off.

"I'm his friend!" Carla stated, loud and bold.

"You're also a cutter," Fred Hammond responded savagely.

Too late, Carla brought her hands behind her back to hide the evidence. She knew they would never take her seriously from this moment onward. She would have to force the issue. Not exactly her style.

William Derek began to pat the chair down. What is he looking for, weapons of mass destruction? Carla wondered. A smile, arrogant as it reached the man's eyes, told her that he had found what he was looking for. Holding up a half-empty bottle of vodka, he asked, "How much? Today?"

"I, ah, I'm afraid I can't help you," Sandstone replied. His eyes fell on Carla, open wide with helplessness. "I honestly don't know."

"Look. What is it exactly that you want us to do?" Hammond asked, his voice heavy with exasperation.

"I don't know. Could you just make the pain go away? I'm not used to pain, especially this much—this kind."

"Come on, Sandstone," Hammond continued. "You've been on these streets for years. We've given you dozens of rides to the hospital."

"You know, the hospital won't be happy to see you," his partner chipped in.

"Maybe you're right," Sandstone said, and he slumped deeper into his chair.

"No! That is not acceptable." Carla was as surprised as everybody else by her sudden outburst. The two paramedics exchanged resigned stares and shrugged their shoulders. Feeling somewhat chastised by her pushiness, they had the stretcher out and beside Sandstone in a well-rehearsed maneuver. Carla bent down to help them lift

Sandstone. His cry of pain tore at her heart. She looked back at the wheelchair seat when they placed him in the ambulance, and Carla's stomach did a back flip that threatened to empty it. Dead maggots floated in a pool of urine and blood in the seat.

The above is an excerpt from *For the Love of Death*, a novel I was getting ready to shop around. While the book is fiction, the character Sandstone was inspired by an actual person, a cantankerous man with a beautiful full gray beard and long white hair. He was also intelligent and cursed with a taste for demon rum. A contagious sense of humor and sardonic wit, born from the ironies and cruel detours of life, were his drawing cards. He lived on our streets years ago; his wheelchair was his mobile place of residence. The incident described above was inspired by the last time I had him taken to the hospital.

A few days after the incident, I found him back on the streets. His flowing hair and signature beard were both missing. Also gone was the arrogant pride that hid his personal despair over a life sentence in a wheelchair. He sat low in his wheelchair, his eyes failing to rise when I approached him. He mumbled to me that they had cut his hair and beard off as punishment for going there. I tried to offer another possibility: Perhaps it was a medical call. He let me know what I could do with that explanation.

More importantly, he was still in pain and not feeling well. To me, he looked like death warmed over. He refused my offer of another try at the hospital. After much pleading, all I could get out of him was his willingness to think about it. Sandstone taught me a valuable lesson that day. The doors that lead to help and hopefully a better life can only be closed so many times before the one in need stops trying to walk through them. In fact, to save the remnants of a fragile ego, the needy pretend that they no longer care. A hardened life view, sometimes an arrogant persona, develops to protect the sense of self. It is a self-defense mechanism.

I remember telling Sandstone I would look him up the next day; hopefully he would change his mind and allow me to place the call. The call I received the next morning was not the one I wanted. His body, folded over in his wheelchair like a broken doll, was found on lower State Street. It was cold, and he had died some time during the night and had remained fallen over like that. I often wondered how many people had passed him, not realizing that he was dead.

This is a simple story, perhaps one without a meaning, except that I remember that colorful man from the streets from a long time ago. Perhaps there are others who remember him. There aren't many of us left from the old days. A number of unique people have come and gone from our streets. But as long as the memory of Sandstone lives, he lives. None of us can say that we have any further claim on life than that. In the end, perhaps that is the great leveling agent that unites us all. Knowing that we leave only memories behind when Death claims his due should humble us all, reminding us it is not the monetary things that measure us but what people remember of us. Were we kind and helpful to the less fortunate, or judgmental and mean in spirit?

An Outbreak of Death

Noozhawk.com, 1-28-10
Three homeless people, two men and a woman, died over the weekend, five people without homes within the last three weeks. My sadness for these people's deaths is equally matched by my dismay over some of the cold-hearted responses, including the suggestion that the homeless should die: "Let the thinning begin." Can't everyone simply respect sadness over the waste of precious life? Of course some homeless made poor life choices, but that is no excuse for callous responses. Can any of us be so arrogant as to be assured that our sons and daughters, our brothers and sisters or parents will never become homeless? Is it ever right for someone to die alone, cold, wet, frightened?

As for James, at least the sounds of the angry guns and horrifying memories of Vietnam are now silenced. I'm not sure dying homeless and alone in I.V. was the "welcome home" he was looking for.

An Alarming Update
Multiple sources have told me that the circumstances of the woman's body indicate that a crime was likely committed at some time before, during, or after death. Attorneys Emily and Joe Allen

have been hired to help ensure the rights and safety of other homeless women. If allegations are true, the perpetrator of such a heinous crime must be brought to justice.

On my first day back from vacation I was handed the following news: a client had been drugged and raped. A car had run off the freeway and hit a man sleeping along the freeway, and another client had hung herself after checking out of the shelter. Where should I place my anger and pain? How do I share this reality with those not caught up in this insanity? If we don't expose our community to the tragedy of the streets, who will? Who, in the end, will stand by the dispossessed in a city framed with so much wealth? Again I find that the complexity of emotional truths is better dissected in fiction than in the linear world that tethers nonfiction.

Innocence Betrayed

Santa Barbara Anthology, When We Were Young, Adulthood, 2000, A Community of Voices

There are certain advantages to being a precocious two-and-a-half-year-old. Take, for example, the stroller that I currently sit in. It is shiny and new, the cool three-wheel variety. It makes jogging easy for my mom. And it doubles as a status symbol. I imagine it cost a pretty penny, but then, I'm worth it. At least according to my mom and dad. People, in general, are friendly. Few harsh words are directed my way. In my household, hunger and physical pain are kept at bay. That makes the current situation that I find myself in disquieting.

Here I sit, bundled against the cold winter wind in my blue hand-knit blanket with matching booties and hat. Lower State Street is busy, boisterous and cheerful on this Friday night. The nightclubs, bars, and restaurants are full of carefree people and fast cash. The sidewalk is congested with a devil-may-care crowd, mostly young. My dad is in the bakery, keeping a practiced eye on me through the big window while he buys me apple juice.

But I am not alone; across from me, my companion sits. A steady stream of people separates us. He is different than most people I see now. He sits like stone, still and glassy-eyed. Like me, he has troubled bladder control. Even from this distance I can smell his urine, see the stain on his pants. I figure he must be cold. He wears only a thin, worn shirt and wet pants. Socks alone enclose his feet. Unlike mine, his have holes in them and smell of rancid decay. They are also bloody. What I can see of his left leg is grossly swollen.

Unlike my stroller, his stroller is old and battered. Plastic bags hang from the back. They look like they hold clothes, lumpy bread, and a half-empty bottle of clear gin.

"Wino! Bum!" a young man says to my companion across the way. His words are trailed by his companions' laughter. I turn my nose up. They smell of booze. The meanness and harsh tone of the young man's words frighten me. The callous laughter of his friends saddens me. Maybe the words and laughter are the cause of the pain deeply etched on the man's sagging, leathery face.

I remember Dad telling Mom, "Alcoholism is a disease." Yet here this sick man sits, deathly still in front of me. Is he being punished because he's sick? Will I be cast out if I get a cold? Will people scurry past me with downcast eyes should I contract the flu? Or are only adults treated so cruelly for their sickness? I'm confused, and that scares me.

My whimpers turn to a hearty cry caused by the terrifying thought of abandonment. Dad rushes over, sticks a bottle in my mouth, and casts a nervous glance at my new friend. I watch a woman deposit a dollar bill in the man's begging cup. She quickly rushes on, sadness pulling at her eyes. I look back when my dad hurries the stroller in and out of pedestrian traffic.

I turn in time to see someone steal my friend's cup. They're stealing his money! I watch as my friend slides out of his wheelchair and hits the ground with a soft thump. He has become a discarded heap that is to be stepped over and avoided.

I wail louder in fright and shame. No longer am I hell-bent on joining this new world or in quite such a hurry to grow up.

A Father's Grief

(Based on an excerpt from my novel, Indecent Times, a Story of Redemption)
"Horsing Around." 1998, Santa Barbara Anthology

Joy hesitated, her hand raised in front of yet another nondescript door. She closed her eyes as war weariness enveloped her body, leaching what little physical stamina she had left. She opened her eyes, narrowed them in an attempt to force her concentration, and knocked.

The knock initiated the by-now familiar routine. The door rattled on its loose hinges, the non-response followed by a louder knock from Joy that finally brought forth a response.

"Frank's not here."

Joy's own response was hesitant, uncertain, because something in the voice denoted suppressed emotions, a warning of some kind that something was wrong.

"Then I need to speak to you," Joy said as she stiffened her body to prepare for any eventuality.

"No! Just go away, will you!"

Joy took a step back and studied the door. She cast a worried look around. The voice within was angry, hurt.

"I, ah, I can't do that," Joy stated with more courage than she felt. "Please open the door. I need ..."

"Why should I?" the unseen voice challenged back.

"Because I hate talking through closed doors! Whadaya think? Jesus Christ, I'm a nurse with the County ... open the damn door, will ya?"

Joy struggled to relax her body; rigid neck muscles began to send pain waves breaking into her head. She rubbed her eyes, hoping to dislodge the tiredness that aged them ten years.

"Come on!" she yelled as she slammed her foot into the door, threatening to liberate the screws from the door's hinges.

"Can't you just leave me alone?" The voice took on a plaintive quality.

Joy stood still; the voice made her feel unexpectedly guilty, made her want to turn and walk away. A heavy sigh announced that as much as she suddenly wanted to, her duty stated otherwise.

"I'm sorry ... I wish I could, but I can't. You need to let me come in."

"All right." The voice had taken on a soft, wounded tone. "It's open. Come in."

Joy reached for the handle and then paused. Her muscles tensed even more; an uneasy feeling told her that the hidden voice was heavily laden with despair, an overwhelming sense of sadness.

Joy sucked up her courage, opened the door, and cautiously walked in. The room was dirty. Filthy might have been a better adjective. The wash sink to her left had two inches of greenish-black water in it. The foul smell was one of pugnacious rot. An annoying drip from the faucet added its charm to this palace of gloom and doom.

Rockers with green- and red-spiked hair, dressed in torn clothes and screaming obscenities, glared down from posters pinned to the walls. A lone dresser stood off to one side, its drawers partially pulled out, revealing clothes that had been hastily and sloppily put away. Skateboard and rock magazines, along with fantasy comic books, littered the floor. Fast food containers and partially empty beer bottles struggled to claim space of their own among the clutter on the floor.

She had been in scores of rooms worse off than this. But the truly odd thing about the room was the man sitting on the bed. The bed, of course, was unmade, with dirty sheet and a green surplus Army blanket bunched up to one side. The man sat alone, holding a small cardboard box.

Joy guessed the man to be in his mid- to late-forties. He wore a soft black sweater, gray slacks, and brown penny loafers. His brown hair was peppered with gray. Reading glasses rested on the bridge of his nose. A shaggy, well-worn stuffed horse that he had pulled from the box sat on his lap.

The hardness in Joy's face began to melt away as an inkling, a dreaded premonition, of the drama that was about to unfold tugged at her conscience.

"You don't live here, do you?" Joy asked with a gentle, quiet voice.

"No."

"Frank? Is this his room? Does he live here?" Joy asked respectfully.

"Yes," the fragile voice answered back.

"Is he, ah, due back soon?" Joy asked as she inched forward.

The man bit his lip, lowered his head, and shook it no.

"Is he coming back?" she asked, struggling to get the words past the lump that had lodged itself at the base of her throat.

The man's hands trembled, the toy horse shook, and his eyes turned red from the effort he made to maintain self-control.

Joy swallowed hard, forcing the lump in her throat to the pit of her stomach where it splashed into an acid bath. Her eyes closed briefly against the resulting pain.

"And Frank would be ...?" she asked. She rushed the question out but was still unable to say the words before her voice broke with emotions.

"He is ... was ... my son," the man said in a simple voice.

Joy pinched her lips painfully together at the expected answer. Her taut neck muscles and sore lips, plus the acid furnace that seconded as her stomach, sent her body into a whole new dimension of pain.

"I'm sorry," Joy stated as mildly as she could through her ragged breath. She tried to slow it down, but to no avail.

"No, it is I who should apologize. Please forgive me," the man stated in a low, raw voice that told Joy that his struggle for self-control was anything but over. "My name's Larry Hazzard. I've come to pack up a few things."

Larry's eyes swept the room as if seeing it for the first time. His eyes narrowed and shed a single tear that ran down his cheek.

"Most of it's garbage I could care less about. But this ..."

Joy followed Larry's line of sight to the scruffy horse that had seen better days. Larry's eyes filled with tears as he fought a battle for control of his devastated emotions.

"I'm sorry to have to ask you this, but I need to know ... For the sake of others. I take it your son ... has ..." Joy faltered as her voice *gave out. She took a deep breath, at least one that passed as one, then continued, "has recently passed away."*

"A week ago today—endocardial infection."

"Once again, I'm sorry. I've had, um, dozens of patients die from that," Joy said as she attempted to share the emotional overload.

Of course what she meant was that junkies by the score died from bacterial contaminated needles. This one particular bacterium had a perverse fondness for the aorta valve of the heart. It would lodge there and eat its host; the person would bleed to death if not diagnosed in time.

"So am I ..."

The words of the grieving father brought Joy back to the here and now.

"So was his mother. She couldn't make it down here ... Hasn't gotten out of bed since ..." Larry punctuated the unfinshed sentence with a heavy sigh.

Joy looked sharply at Larry Hazzard. She detected in his speech a need to vent, a need to question, a need to figure out the whys, when there were no answers.

"Frank was mentally ill. He had his first psychotic break in his sophomore year. At first his mother and I just assumed it was typical teenage rebellion, you know—he quit bathing, no longer cared what he looked like or how he dressed. Then we assumed the mood swings, the depression, were teenage angst. Hadn't we all gone through that?

"Then the hard part came when we finally accepted the truth and tried to get him help. Unfortunately, he had begun to treat, ah, to medicate himself with street drugs. And the mental health system and then the hospitals refused to treat him, to hospitalize him, till he had been off the drugs for six months to a year."

A suffocating silence invaded the room, crushing the breath out of Joy. Finally a sigh came from the depths of Larry's soul to contest the void. He found the courage to continue.

"Do you know what it's like to ask for, no, plead for help for your son, only to be told he has to stop his own self-medication for half a year before they would help? We pleaded, we threatened to sue, but they said it was a state mandate not to treat the dually inflicted.

That's the term they used. That's what they called my son because he had two problems, drugs and mental illness, instead of just one."

Once again Larry faltered, or maybe he just rested, before he could continue.

"For the last five years we watched as our son died and a stranger came to live with us. It may have been the same body, but it wasn't him. Midnight calls from the police came for joy riding, driving under the influence, petty shoplifting. And the ever-infamous 647F, being under the influence," Larry stated with bitterness.

"How did he end up here, with that particular infection?" Joy was forced to ask.

A look of shame swamped Larry's face. "Because ..." He was forced to stop till he could stem the flow of tears that had begun to silently fall. "Because I sent him here. He had begun to run with a fast drug crowd. No, that's not fair to him. He began to be used by a drug crowd. Frank was gullible, had no judgment. When he wasn't high on crack, the demons haunted him with suicidal despair. And when he was high, the demons taunted him, till only more crack would finally silence them. The druggies began to use him as a mule. That's what the police called it ... You know, get him high and have him deliver the drugs for them. That way, if he got caught, they were still in the clear."

Larry laughed bitterly at the insanity of it all before he continued. "See, they only had to pay him in rocks ... in rocks, for God's sake! No withholding taxes, no retirement or disability plans. Cheap and efficient."

"But that still doesn't ..."

"Can you imagine what it's like to hold your child in your arms while he literally tries to tear the skin off his arms to get at the coke bugs underneath? And what it's like to hold him when the voices from his mad world come looking for him, to drag him back into that hell of a psychotic, delusional world? And we promised, his mother and I, that tomorrow would be different. That we would get him help first thing in the morning, the next day. And all our pleas for help were always answered the same way. 'When he's clean and off the drugs.' How in God's name was he supposed to get off the stuff when that

was the only medication that he had? How could they have turned us down time after time? How?" Larry begged Joy for an answer.

She dropped her eyes in shame, shame over a medical profession in denial as much as any one of her patient-junkies. Shame for the morally right answer that was never found.

In a lower voice drenched in guilt and shame of his own, Larry continued. "So I sent Frank here, to this city, four months ago. I couldn't take it anymore. Five years we've struggled with this. Five years with no life of our own! Always terrified when the phone rang. All I wanted was some peace and happiness. Do you know how long it had been since we laughed? Since I had made love to my wife?

"So I sent him away for my own sanity. I paid the first month's rent at another motel. Frank went into the Welfare Department to apply for GR. He told them that he needed help, that he was addicted to crack and that he was a schizophrenic. What do you think they did? They put him into this hotel, where half the guests are either addicted or making a living off those who are. But he did get off the crack. Frank found salvation in heroin and in the needle. He also found death there."

Tears began to flow freely down both Joy's and Larry's faces. Joy wondered what kind of a world this had become. Larry wondered how he would ever be able to live with so much pain and guilt.

"I'm sorry. I really am sorry. I'll leave you alone to finish whatever business you have here. And if I can be of any help ...?" Joy began to offer.

With heightened expectations, pleading for an answer, for absolution, Larry cut in. "What else could I have done? Tell me it wasn't wrong of me, selfish of me, to send my son away, was it? Five years! Five years of living in a nightmare. We, I, tried! I honestly tried! Dear God, tell me I didn't send my son to his death. Tell me I didn't kill him."

Larry broke out in loud, soul-wrenching sobs and buried his face in the pathetic little horse. His body rocked with his heavy sobs. Joy quietly backed up and gently dragged the door shut behind her. But she was unable to stop the haunting anguish of a tormented father that shattered through the closed door.

Clergy at the memorial for homeless dead. Summer 2009.

Sculpture by Morris Bear Squire in honor of
the homeless dead. Summer 2009.

Ken Williams and Dr. Lynne Jahnke, better
known as Dr. J on the streets.

Parish Nurse Jan Fadden and Ken Williams.

Name on Memorial Wall. One of hundreds honored who have died on Santa Barbara's streets. Joshua was the youngest.

Modern covered wagon, with all worldly possessions.

Prepared for foul weather.

Downtown Santa Barbara.

A man's castle?

Ross's home—entrance to a public bathroom.
Place of the assault that killed him.

A homeless encampment.

This bus stop where his body was found was Freedom's home.

While the homeless died on the streets, this low-income hotel stood empty for over five years.

Money talks. This empty hole across from the closed, low-income hotel is redevelopment in Santa Barbara.

Entrance to the hole. What work?

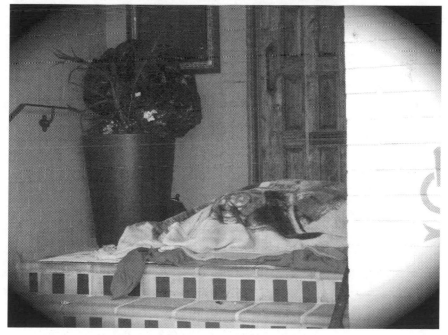

Suffering through a cold and wet night.

A homeless encampment under a bridge.

Where the bodies of two homeless men were found
within twenty-four hours of each other.

Memorial Wall that hangs at the Salvation Army.

The ringleaders of Project Healthy Neighbors.

My partner in crime for Project Healthy Neighbors,
Dana Gamble from Public Health.

A homeless encampment along the railroad tracks and the freeway.

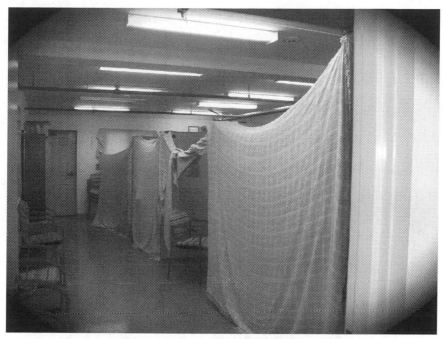

Makeshift interview-examination rooms
for Project Healthy Neighbors.

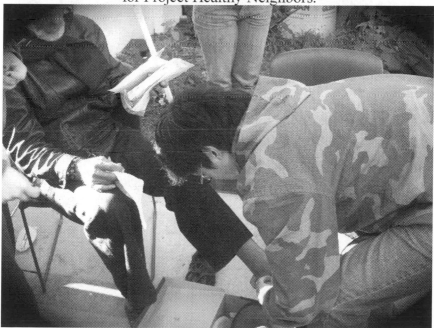

Fitting a new pair of shoes as an incentive for medical
services, including vaccines and TB and HIV testing.

John Buttny and Merryl Brown handing out another incentive for Project Healthy Neighbors: survivor backpacks for the winter.

Book Three

Hope

CHAPTER ELEVEN

The most frequently asked question I get when I give presentations is: what keeps me going after so many years, after so much pain, indifference, and defeat on a hundred fronts? First and foremost, it's my clients. They have given me a thousand-fold payback for whatever I have managed to give them. They have taught me the grace of humility and the beauty of life, to not let others prejudice my own moral outlook and to never give up, even in the face of overwhelming odds. I have seen so much grace under pressure, so much spunk and defiance in the face of overwhelming tragedy, that I am frequently left speechless. Always, and in spite of, or because of, their own struggles, they have shown me the real treasures of life: good health, family, love, friendship, and a belief in the spiritual dimension that they live, not merely profess.

One homeless man, damaged by his lifestyle as well as mental illness, would drop food off to a room-bound mentally ill woman when she isolated herself due to her delusions. He took the time out from surviving on the mean streets to make sure that woman would not go hungry because of the very disease that condemned him to the streets. I can't think of a better illustration of love and caring from one human being to another.

And then there are the good citizens of Santa Barbara, those who have consistently come forward with advice, encouragement, and money for projects that without their backing would have been impossible. Over the last several years they have given me many gifts during the Christmas season to take to those on the streets; the holiday season can seem particularly cruel to those isolated to the streets by their disabilities. Oftentimes it is the grace of these good people that balances the pain that comes with the job. The tradition started humbly years ago.

Ken Williams

Angels on State Street

Santa Barbara Independent, 12-98

It was damn cold; I watched the steam curl upward from the coffee cup I held in my hands. The young sun lit the sky but had not yet broken through the horizon. The coldness of the bitter holiday season morning cut through my leather jacket like daggers. I wrapped both hands more tightly around the paper cup, trying to ward off the pain. My breath was visible as I watched the homeless man across the street from me. I had seen him many times before, sitting at the same bus stop, behind an invisible glass wall that separated him from the other citizens of the city. The man always wore the same inscrutable frown—not exactly hostile, but enough doubt remained to inspire caution.

I knew better than to judge him harshly, knowing that many homeless mentally ill adopted tough exteriors as a mode of self-protection. "You can't hurt me anymore," their look conveys. "You've hurt me as much as any human being can be hurt, and I still exist. Bloodied, bowed, yet I exist." That's what my rational mind told me, having gained that knowledge from twenty years of working the streets. Still, my emotions, my not-so-hidden fears and paranoias, told me otherwise. What did I really know about him? How deeply did I actually believe the speeches I had given and the thousands of words I had written over the years, trying to dispel the hateful stereotypes that Hollywood makes a killing on—the psychopathic killer, the mentally ill person as an abstraction that runs rampant through the studios—in make-believe land?

I know. I have seen the violence that steel and flames can do to human flesh, to the human body. I try to keep those images buried, or at least contained, so as not to let them run my life. But they're always there, as is the reality of the harsh jungle that America's streets can be.

Maybe it was the cold, the pain, that finally forced my hand. Either I got on with the business at hand, crossed the street, and dealt with him, or I got on with my rounds. I bunched up my shoulders, dug the twenty-dollar bill from my pocket, made sure it was folded into a neat, small bundle tucked into the palm of my free hand. A quick glance assured me that no threat of a jaywalking ticket could be used as an excuse to turn and walk away. In fact, there was no one else out on the street this cold morning, just my unknown friend and my known fears.

The man didn't see me; his back was to me. I made sure to cross the street far enough down from him so he would see me approach and not be taken by surprise. His hooded eyes immediately landed on me and stayed on me. He watched me come closer with some concern. His eyes darkened with questions, bordering on apprehension, as he waited for me to make the first move.

"I'd like to give you a little something for Christmas," I heard myself say. At least my voice sounded normal, or as normal as it ever gets in this business. Frosty, visible breath marked the space between us. To my surprise, his smile was immediate and friendly as we reached out to shake hands. He looked down at the folded twenty that had passed from me to him. His smile brightened; an easy "Thank you" in an exotic accent was extended to me on his fogged breath.

A clumsy "You're welcome" helped hide some of the shame I felt for having had the feelings of a moment before. I hesitated, wishing there was something more to be said, some other connection to be made between this gentleman of the street and me. But I had been here too many times before. The lack of resources for the mentally ill homeless in particular and the homeless in general were burned feverishly into my consciousness. Besides, I had others I needed to run down before Christmas.

I had been sent on a mission of mercy by two foster angels of the streets: two working people, not rich by any stretch of the imagination. Like most of us who work in Santa Barbara, not even well-off. Two working people who struggled hard to survive but somehow remembered what the true meaning of Christmas was about. They had come to me with a proposition. They would give me all the money they would have spent on family and friends for gifts, if I could give the money in small amounts to the poorest of the poor, reaching out to those lost souls who would greatly appreciate and benefit from a gift of the heart. In return, I made a pledge to myself that I would not feed the addiction of those suffering greatly from their curse. I would not enhance the profits of either the pusher or the corner liquor store, which at times seemed to be one and the same.

This simple, gracious gift from the heart sent me on a two-week journey to every nook and cranny where those criminalized, victimized, ostracized, and abused by an often callous and indifferent city and its power elite live. I found myself in a foot race with the police, who seemed on a mission to clean up the downtown shopping corridor in their belief, or more likely on orders, that the good citizens of the community would be put off by the heart-wrenching sight of the lost souls and forego spending their money on gifts.

I distributed the money, and, in return, I received more precious, invaluable lessons in life, love, and humility than I could ever hope to purchase. I wish to thank those who have once again so graciously been my teachers:

To the man who faced death this year and learned the hard way the cost of the color of his skin and the lack of a bank account.

To the lady of the streets who always had an encouraging word for those worse off than she was. I'm not sure who could be much worse off than someone who slept outside during the harsh winter.

To the gentleman of the streets who came to me when he saw others, predators really, who were abusing a mentally ill person who somehow survived the winter literally on the streets.

To the waif-like homeless man, more like a boy really, who was afraid that the police would want to know how someone of his limited means and affliction could afford the rain slick and sweatshirt I gave him. I gave him my business card and told him to tell them to call me if there was any trouble. Just so we know hatred is an equal-opportunity despoiler, I had to get the clothes in a smaller size so the man who camps next to him wouldn't steal them, as he had this person's other belongings.

To the man driven to despair by what he felt was the constant attempt to run him and others like him out of town.

To those I gave to who suffered from the aches and pains of arthritis and other degenerative diseases, who were forced to spend the killer winter in the Armory, in cars, and behind bushes. I can't even begin to imagine the pain you must have gone through.

To the man with the lost look, sunken face, wild beard, shoulder-length matted hair, and clothes so old and dirty they had not only holes in them but also sheen to them. Your shocked look so quickly turned to the warmest smile I had seen in a long time.

And to all the other mentally ill homeless who had that tortured look in their eyes, not only from the disease but the hurt and pain caused by those who fear them and refuse to see them as people but only as transients and bums.

To you who had the look of a deer caught in the hunter's light at night, the look of a survivor of man's inhumanity to man.

I wish to thank the two foster-angels of the streets. You not only helped those you intended to help, but me as well. I had begun to become too focused on those in this community who wish to run the homeless out of town; those who find the poor a nuisance and an inconvenience to their grand plans for our community; those in the business community who see profit as the only yardstick by which to measure progress; by the political elite who neglected to save the low-income housing of the SROs—Single Residential Occupant hotels on their watch. My heart had begun to turn cold and bitter under that focus.

You reminded me of the other side of Santa Barbara: the people who, out of love, work and volunteer at the Salvation Army, the Rescue Mission, the Women's Shelter, the Rape Crisis Center, the Drop-in Center, Storyteller, the Faulding Hotel, the Community Soup Kitchen, Transition House, and the scores of other projects that define the soul of Santa Barbara, of those businesses and the few politicians who know that matters of the heart and soul need to have a place at the table and act accordingly.

And finally, you reminded me that a community is a complex entity that covers a wide spectrum of people. The poor and homeless are part of that community, and we neglect their well-being at the expense of what we define as our spirituality, our morality, and our religion. Thank you for having sent me on a modern odyssey into an American jungle, to emerge having stared down the true heart of darkness.

Once, on Christmas Eve as the sun begun to set, I found a man setting up his sleeping bag on the lawn of the library. No other homeless or others were around. The library was closed, as were all the stores. The streets were eerily deserted of both cars and pedestrians. Santa Barbara never seemed so depopulated or so lonely.

I walked up to the man and gave him a twenty, telling him to get a good Christmas dinner. Walking away, I heard him mumble something incomprehensible: A curse? A blessing? Did he know it was even Christmas? Or in the middle of all his delusions, did some part of him connect with the offer? Did he realize someone cared enough to give me the money to give to him, a token of their love? A sense of profound aloneness pressed down on me when I walked away.

Another time I had given a little boy five dollars at the organic market on State Street for a small angel that he was selling. Walking back to my truck, I couldn't shake the feeling that whatever money he made that Tuesday before Christmas was what he and his mom would have to spend. Retracing my steps, I walked back and gave him more money. His mother, who had been sitting on the curb watching over her son, suddenly broke down and began to cry, hard tears washing over fallen dreams.

Below, are notes from Christmas 2009 about some of the people who received special attention. This list also gives a good snapshot of who makes up our homeless population and why it is such a crime that they do so. (A few have been deleted, which is why some numbers are missing.)

1. Woman in wheelchair

3. Woman with a pushcart overflowing with stuff

4. 75-year-old man—filthy jacket, dirty shoes

5. 50-ish man, no shoes, only socks; shopping cart; physically disabled

7. Man, 30s, just out of hospital today—food poisoning

8. Male, late 20s, wearing a dirty field coat; black plastic bags filled with stuff. Had to convince him to take gift. Extremely polite and shy

9. Mentally ill woman needed money for Xmas gift for her daughter

11. 44-year-old mentally ill man, staying at shelter and streets; shy

13. Mid-40s Latino man, recently out of hospital for severe suicidal depression

14. 64-year-old deaf mute. A real heartbreaker

15. Woman staying at shelter, severe depression; sits in chair all day and stares at the ground

16. 50-year-old woman, severe back injury

17. Disabled woman, mid-50s, living in van

19. Severe bipolar M.I. man with lots of stuff—State Street

21. Mid-40s disabled woman, State St., 7:30 AM

22. 60-ish male, State St., 7:35 AM

23. 50-ish man, disabled

24. HIV positive woman

25. 50-ish mentally ill woman

26. Latino man, 70s, living in his car

27. Mid-40s, bi-polar

28. Diabetic blind woman, vet, afraid of being homeless

29. Mid-30s woman, severe health issues

30. Crippled man in wheelchair, mid-30s

31. Mid-50s woman with severe back injury

32. Homeless woman, mid-50s

33. Man, mid-60s, very delusional, 10:30 AM, State St.

34. Tall man, beard, no shoes; very mentally ill, 10:40 AM, State St.

35. Large man with beard, 11:00 AM State St. When asked how long he has been homeless: "Forever"

36. 40-year-old woman, just out of hospital—food poisoning

37. 60-year-old woman, State St.

38. 50-ish woman, obviously crippled, living in van

39. Family: man, woman, and six-month-old baby; State St.

40. Mentally ill young man with cat: "addicted to roasted chicken"

41. Tall man, no teeth, 7:30 AM State St.

42. Tall man, infected wound; just lost the car he was sleeping in; 7:50 library

43. Pregnant woman losing her housing

44. 44-year-old woman, diabetic and dialysis

45. 40-ish disabled man, very obese

46. 50-ish woman, bent over in extreme pain, crying; lives in beaten down van

47. Young man, very mentally ill; wouldn't make eye contact. Cacique St., 10:15

49. Diabetic man, mid-40s

50. Homeless teens trying to get home for Christmas

51. Couple sleeping in station wagon

52. Woman, mid-30s, severe stomach problems

53. 50-ish vet

54. 55-year-old woman abandoned by her husband to rent a motel room

55. Older man with full beard, very nice and polite

56. Single father with kids, one who is severely disabled

58. Very shy, depressed man, mid-30s, 10:30, State St.

59. Older woman, walking in obvious pain, living in tool shed; 10:30, State St.

60. Woman, mid-40s, plastic bags, mentally ill; State St., 10:45

61. Woman, mid-50s, walking in hard pain

62. Mid-30s, severely depressed man with five-year-old daughter

63. Woman, mid-50s in wheelchair, recent surgery

65. Homeless man, mid-60s, on bike, sleeps on beach

66. Young woman, tall, wearing a sleeping bag; 7:15, State St.

67. Short, mentally ill man wearing a woman's coat; 7:20, Chapala

69. Physically disabled man—recent heart surgery

70. Mentally ill man

71. Mentally ill man staying at the RM

72. Paralyzed man in wheelchair; Canon Perdido and State, 8:45

73. Mid-40s man, very cold, State St., 9:15.

74. Young man hit by car, hurt leg

76. Mother and two daughters, shelter

77. Tall man—very paranoid

78. Late-50s man, stroke this year

79. Severely disabled woman in wheelchair

80. Mid-50s, very mentally ill man; wrapped in a blanket. State St., 7:20 AM

81. 60-ish vet

82. 60-ish man living in his van cooking breakfast

83. Old woman with top-heavy grocery cart with tons of stuff piled high; State St., 9:30

84. Woman, shoulder-length gray hair, navy coat, very mentally ill; front of City Hall, 9:40

85. Mentally ill woman washing clothes in front of Borders

86. Heavy-set man wearing a poncho, very mentally ill

87. Mom and dad and baby living in car; out of baby formula

88. Very dirty 40-ish man digging through trash can on State St., severely depressed. 7:45 AM

91. Homeless man who will get his two kids today; needs presents

92. 30-ish man, very mentally ill, skinny, talking to himself

93. Woman, early 40s, mentally ill, blue hoodie pulled down tight

95. Woman in wheelchair, 30s

97. Older man, gray beard, signing on State St.

99. Very tall mentally ill man, eating out of trash can

Casa Rosa was a home for homeless women with substance abuse problems and their children. It's a rule, written in stone in the recovery community, that women struggling to kick habits must be separated from their children in order to successfully deal with their addictions. It is a rule that I find myself at odds with. To me, pulling a woman away from her children in order for her to work on her own substance abuse problems only adds guilt, adding another layer that further pushes her towards the numbing chemical agents that she has been conditioned to seek out when stressors become overwhelming. Shame and guilt on top of one another build till it becomes impossible for her to face a sober future. And the issues of bonding and mothering skills are never even talked about or, more devastatingly, worked on.

Many of the women-girls had come from broken or abusive homes. How is the cycle to be altered without teaching and encouraging them toward a different type of mothering? What they needed was a safe place, a home in every sense of the word, where parenting classes co-exist with the work on their substance abuse issues.

A nurse and I came up with the idea when we got tired of counseling homeless pregnant women that they needed to clean up so as not to damage the unborn. "Fine," they would tell us. Then they would ask where were they supposed to go and live, knowing full well that no place would take them unless they first agreed to give up their babies at birth.

Over coffee we came up with the idea of Casa Rosa. We knew that we would need "seed" money to get it off the ground. Out of the blue, a saintly man, who over the years has donated hundreds of thousands of dollars to the cause of the homeless, asked us to a meeting. Before a handful of homeless advocates, he announced that a business deal had left him with a surplus of fifty thousand dollars and that it was ours to spend as we wanted—even to the extent of just taking a sabbatical off from work and living on his donation. None of us asked for that; instead we all got pet projects funded—Casa Rosa was born with a donation of a few thousand dollars, the seed money for a dream.

The next step was to go after a million and half dollar multi-year federal grant. We found ourselves in competition with the county, which wanted the money for case management. Great idea, except what good was case management when the women were pregnant, addicted, and homeless?

I knew that a social worker and a nurse competing for a grant against an institution such as the county would go nowhere. I needed a game plan to force the county to drop their grant proposal. I went to the newspaper, the *Independent,* with the story of our pie-in-the-sky dream for Casa Rosa. I told about the tragedy of homeless alcoholic and drug-addicted pregnant women with no place to turn for help and about babies damaged by fetal alcohol syndrome and/or born addicted. Mysterious deep pocket donors were alluded to and political connections hinted at; mostly it was a wing and a prayer wrapped inside a bluff, with plenty of wild cards thrown in, but not much beyond that.

Within days of the article, the director of Health Care Services met with me. Not only would he drop their competing bid, but he also graciously gave us support staff to work alongside us.

The next step was to hire a professional grant writer. I spent all the monies that I had received from the funder to do so. Everything from there on would be pure bluff.

While waiting for the feds to determine who would received their blessings, we began to look for a house, a huge potential stumbling block in a community where Not In My Backyard (NIMBism), parochial interests, and sky-high housing and rental prices all frequently delayed such projects by decades. I had been meeting with a local hospital, hoping to entice them into a partnership on Casa Rosa, really hoping that they would take the project over. After stringing me along for several weeks, the CEO finally blew me off, letting me know in no uncertain terms that I must be out of my mind to have ever entertained the notion of a hospital working on such a grandiose project with a mere social worker without departmental backing.

But it was the nature of this dream that nothing stood in its way for very long. Before our last meeting, the CEO had inadvertently shared with me a listing for a house in Montecito that the hospital was looking at for possible acquisition. I borrowed the leaflet, with the name of the reality company and the address of the house in question printed on it.

Out of desperation and the sense of unreality that had become attached to the project, I drove out to the house. Readers should know that Montecito is one of the most exclusive and expensive residential communities in the United States, populated by Hollywood types and old-money wealth.

The house, actually a huge mansion, was unbelievable: brownstone, with large rooms and soaring ceilings, wooden floors, tons of rooms, and a back yard to die for. Its one drawback was that the freeway was just across the street. Before the freeway was built, the grounds had extended all the way to the ocean. We got the grant, rented the house, and brought homeless women and their children to live there. We brought the professionals that they needed to them. Childcare, substance abuse recovery classes, prenatal and postnatal care, parenting classes, acupuncture, and so much more was provided—all with dignity, respect, and an ocean of love. Hundreds of women and children cycled through Casa Rosa during the life of the grant. They literally lived among some of the wealthiest citizens of our country, in a mansion they couldn't even begin to fantasize about in their most delusional drug fantasies.

Another time, after becoming discouraged by seeing children in a homeless soup kitchen, I approached a fairly conservation foundation with the idea of a children's soup kitchen. Martiza's Cocina was conceived and funded and off and running at Casa Rosa mere months after the concept was born. I remember one CEO asking me if I was serving undocumented children. I could tell that he felt badly, but he was asking the question that I'm sure he had been asked a hundred times by foundation donors on different projects he had backed. I gave him the answer that I knew was already in his heart: "I don't ask for birth certificates from hungry children. I simply feed them."

A manager at Social Services, though worded slightly differently, expressed the same concern to me—that perhaps the skin color of the children we proposed to feed was problematic. She was concerned that perhaps the timing for the proposal was not right, since some racist's initiative was on the California State ballot. I guess I never thought of a God looking down on us through skin-colored glasses.

A few years before Casa Rosa, I had begun to encounter more than a few mentally ill pregnant and homeless women. Once again I was moved to try and establish a house where such troubled women could reside. AMBR House, A Mother and Baby's Respite, was born. And once again an angel came forward to fund it. AMBR House lasted a year; the project showed me the shortcomings of being an innovator who lacked the critical institutional support to see such projects through. Fortunately, by the time Casa Rosa came to fruition, I had established a friendly relationship with the director of the I.V. Medical Center—yet another saintly man. It was they who managed the program.

Over the years, I have worked with, established, found funding for, or run a variety of programs for homeless families, including the Michael Fund, the No Name Group, and the Oscar Romero Fund, named in honor of the assassinated archbishop of El Salvador who had dared stand with the poor in the face of the right-wing death squads.

I was also one of the founding members of Storyteller, a childcare center for homeless children. One of the memories of that project that always brings a tear of amusement and a tear of heartbreak was a luncheon I attended in the early planning stages. We were all very enthusiastic about the project, idealistic in our purpose. Then reality, or so I thought, settled in. I pulled back my chair, thinking what a waste of time and effort we were engaged in. I knew deep down that once Americans discovered that there were homeless children on our streets, a wave of revulsion and shame would force the politicians to deal with the problem. Unfortunately, my mindset was still lodged in the sixties and the idea that our society had the willpower to seek to abolish that newest affront to our humanity. That luncheon was more than twenty years ago. Since then Storyteller has served thousands of children.

The first organizations in Santa Barbara to face up to the reality of homelessness and try to deal with it were the Salvation Army and Catholic Charities. And that was only because of the two outstanding citizens in our community who ran those organizations: John Jamieson and Rosemary Varsario. They, along with me from Social Services and two Mental Health workers, took up the task that nobody else wanted: to try and coordinate services for the homeless. We were faced with what had become, up till then, a bureaucratic response to the developing crisis of homelessness, which was to deny services any way an agency could, which included referring them back and forth to non-existent services in the hope of discouraging them from ever getting any help.

We operated under the name of The Coordinating Committee for the Homeless Mentally Ill. In time we simplified it by simply calling ourselves the Coordinating Committee for the Homeless. The goal was to identify those endangered by their homeless status:

the mentally ill and physically disabled, children, pregnant women, and women in general. Once we identified them, we then tried to coordinate an outreach plan to secure emergency housing, cash assistance, mental health and medical services, or whatever else it would take to move them off the streets.

As time went by and the stream of homelessness became first a river, then a flood, and finally a deluge, some of us accepted the reality that part of our job had become to simply make people's existence on the streets a little easier, with the ever-receding end goal of moving them off the streets. That might include something as simple as providing a blanket, sleeping bag, poncho, jacket, or a few days of rest in a shelter.

The latter, a few days respite from the streets, may seem the easiest, but in many respects it was the hardest thing to accomplish. Almost all shelters are restricted: some by mandatory alcohol and drug testing that effectively excludes many homeless, including at least half of the mentally ill, who treat their disability with alcohol and/or drugs. And shelters that don't test make beds available only through referral from selected providers. Every shelter wrestles with this problem. I have often spent days looking for a single bed for a homeless man, woman, or child who falls outside the categories that designate the salvageable homeless.

Even in the main homeless shelter, which was partially established to provide for the homeless that none of the other shelters wanted, it was a constant battle to keep the doors open to those damaged by mental illness and substance abuse. The man who had originally funded Casa Rosa played a critical role in this regard when he linked his donations to the shelter to the condition that I have access to emergency beds there.

Often the service providers themselves were the highest hurdles to the homeless shelters and services. They had become shell-shocked and then jaded by the oceans of human misery that we found ourselves swimming in. It was a constant state of war, with more casualties than available services. For all too many, it became easier to exclude whole categories of people rather than look an individual in the eye and share his pain, her despair, and try and maintain either a professional relationship with him, or at least a friendship, when no shelter beds were available. It was far easier to blame the victim for her plight. Exclusion offered one way of protecting service workers from going crazy amidst all the human suffering and death that surrounds someone who works the streets.

A fond yet bittersweet memory is the day when two funders asked me out to lunch. Sensing my tension or seeing the sadness in my eyes, they asked what was wrong. I informed them that when no beds were available for him, a gentle homeless man had been beaten to death in front of the Rescue Mission. One of them remembered that when we were in the planning stages for the new shelter, within the conditional use permit I had included a plan for a year-round shelter. Up to that time, we hadn't had the money to run the shelter all year, so except for the four months of the emergency winter shelter season, two hundred beds stood empty while the homeless walked the streets, looking for a place to lay down their weary and tired bodies at night.

The two men were kind enough to offer the money to open up those beds. The shelter expanded from no beds to thirty beds and eventually to the present one hundred beds. Still, one hundred beds remain empty for eight months of the year. Annually we fight battles with those who would like to shut us down or at least shut down or move our soup kitchen elsewhere—in the middle of the largest recession in eighty years. When did feeding the poor and homeless become such a controversial issue?

In the end it is the struggles and the triumphs of the homeless themselves that give us the strength to keep going forward and fight for justice. Their impossible struggles and victories in the face of certain death not only leave me in awe but with the strength to fight the never-ending battles on their behalf. Perhaps no story better illustrated this than the following one.

Hope

Unpublished
Are the streets always a death sentence? Does Death always win in the end? My wife warns me about my preoccupation with death.

She blames Vietnam. I lay blame on Death. But she has a point. Too often I see my nemesis winning too many rounds. I need to remind myself of the feistiness of the human spirit, of the incredible will to live. In the end, only God can play God, and no one is without hope. One man's story reminds me that in life there is always hope.

The spring day was warm; bright sunshine promised a good day. The sweet smell of flowering plants and trees and freshly cut grass— renewed life after a long winter—filled the air. The promise was bitterly betrayed when I approached the bandstand. Moses lay like a beached whale, naked in a soiled sleeping bag. An overpowering odor of decay, feces, and urine blanketed the bandstand like a repelling fog. I had been warned about Moses' condition, but the state of the man who lay at my feet shook me. His glistening white belly was hugely distended, telling me that his liver and kidneys were shutting down. His skin was grafted with hideous, weeping sores. Vital organs had ballooned up to the size of grapefruits and shut down.

I bent down next to him, careful not to stain my pants. For the next several minutes we engaged in a deadly philosophical debate about why life was worth living. I told him all the reasons why life is a precious gift and why suicide by drinking, pulling the trigger of a liquid gun, was stupid. We talked about family left behind, the pain they would endure if he refused my offer to call an ambulance. I tried spoon-feeding him soup that I had paid a homie from the park to go and get. He waved off the crackers, reminding me that the salt on them was bad for his liver, that his body would retain even more water than at present. We ended our conversations at a draw, him not sure if a life of pain was worth the effort, me unsure if I had made any progress.

The next day I went back. The only evidence that someone had called the bandstand home hours before were body fluid stains on the floor. I began to search the ivy-covered hill behind, looking for a body. (It wouldn't be the first.) A homie drifting by told me that Moses had agreed to allow the paramedics to take him in late last night. Over the next several weeks, in and out of the hospital, into a van and then hospice, the man the streets knew as Moses became "David" to me.

David was a man who had danced with death for the last several years, but it had not always been so. David was born forty-four years ago in Texas. He was raised there and in Arizona on working ranches and farms. Through hard work, he was able to own his own ranch and, according to him, made "too much money" by the age of twenty-two. Along with all that money he picked up baggage, one his damaged liver, which he blamed on a concoction of chemicals used in modern ranching and farming. The other was a propensity for drugs and alcohol; coke fell like winter snow, and alcohol flowed like spring rains.

The ranch and family were the first things to fall victim to his fast lifestyle. Having lost both, David ran hard and fast, but never far or fast enough to outrun himself or his addictions. Finally David found himself a dying alcoholic on the streets of Santa Barbara, which he has called home on and off for the last twenty years.

Along the way, he picked up the street name Moses, for his tendency to try to take care of other street dwellers. He was particularly famous for feeding them. One of the more wild and reliable stories is about him "using" the kitchen of one of the homeless shelters after hours to make sandwiches for the homeless. He would write their names, their likes and dislikes, and any medical conditions that might relate to their nutritional needs on the outside of the lunch bags that he assembled. He was finally discovered after months of doing this when he went back once, having forgotten a diabetic's lunch.

A little over two years ago David hit bottom. His home was the bandstand at the park by the harbor where I found him. When he was finally taken into the hospital, it took them weeks to drain off the pounds of excess body fluids that his liver was no longer able to process. Fighting through intolerable pain, David refused to surrender to death, which had constantly shadowed him like a groupie. A strong belief in life and an engaging personality enabled him to fight death to a standstill, even though its seductive siren song had come close to enticing David to give up and cross over.

David is a man who looks proudly on his three daughters and eight grandkids, on the fact that he helped others even when he himself was slipping rapidly downhill. When someone first meets this man, his life and death struggle is not readily apparent. Instead you might mistake him for a vacationing retiree, a young one, but a retiree nonetheless. Loud Hawaiian shirts, Bermuda shorts, and sandals play their part, as does the tan, portly body that at first hides his journey well. But his struggle and pain are branded into his chocolate-colored eyes. They have looked into the abyss that we all must confront in the end and saw death staring back.

In the end, alcoholism always claims its victim, as does the human condition. Few are able to confront their journey's end, fight back, and with dignity reclaim life. David is one such man, and I am both greater and lesser because of it.

One day I received a phone call from my older son Sal, who lived in New York at the time. He told me he had just gotten back from a sixty-block excursion. Being strapped for money, he had the good fortune of finding a five-dollar bill on the street. Adding that to the two dollars he had on him, he had just enough for a lunch special: a sandwich, chips, and soda. Approaching a store, he saw a scruffy homeless man digging through a trash can looking for food. Good luck was with the man that day; he found a leftover drink. Bad luck also visited him, when a man exiting the store shouting for the other man "to get a job." My son came to the defense of the homeless man, telling the irate citizen that he should "get a soul."

Sal went into the store, bought the lunch special, and gave it to the man. The grateful man told my son, "No one has ever done something like that for me before." If my son goes on and makes millions and has a brilliant career (which I'm sure that he will), he will never do himself prouder than bringing a measure of compassion and love to another person like he did that day. Nor will he ever make me prouder.

I know that there's always the danger of judging others, of not remembering the humble grace that my homeless clients have taught and retaught me over the years. It's dangerous to succumb to self-righteousness when one fights for a moral principal, an insidious manifestation that robs opponents of their humanity, even when it's wounded.

CHAPTER TWELVE

The Epidemic that Wasn't

Noozhawk.com, 2-10-08 and Santa Barbara Independent, 2-14-08

For years I have written that the homeless are not an entity unto themselves. None of us are. They are our brothers and sisters, our mothers and fathers, our children, and our neighbors. They are as much a part of our community as anyone else. We ignore them at our own peril, both spiritually and otherwise. I would also argue that by ignoring the tragedy of homelessness, we not only fail our faith and spiritual beliefs, but we also compound the problem until solutions become tangled and expensive.

The crisis of treating the dually diagnosed is one example of this tragic outcome. We not only have to treat the mental problems of those who suffer from schizophrenia, bipolar, and other diseases of the mind but their addictions; when left untreated, those afflicted turn to drugs and alcohol to self-medicate their symptoms. It would have been so much more humane and less costly to treat their mental problems before drugs were involved. The tuberculosis scare that we are currently dealing with is another such example. But workable, cost-effective solutions are also part of this story. In this potentially scary article, a bright spot of compassion and foresight is found.

Four years ago, I was having dinner with Dr. Mark Stinson. He was telling me of his experience with the victims of the tsunami that had devastated Indonesia. He also told me of MASH units that the Brazilian military had established in shantytowns to combat third world diseases. I told him I had often dreamed of conducting a mobile medical clinic at the homeless shelter for just such a need. It was agreed that if I organized it, he would come and offer his services.

Before his tragic death last year, Mark did in fact participate in Project Healthy Neighbors I and II.

This year, for Project Healthy Neighbors III, Dr. Andy Gersoff took the lead and was kind enough to offer doctors from the Internal Medicine Residency Program at Cottage Hospital. Under the able supervision of Dr. Lynne Jahnke, these doctors conducted medical screenings for the homeless. HIV testing; inoculations for the flu and pneumonia; mental health, veteran, and social services; substance abuse counseling, and more were offered. Cottage Hospital also provided the tents and nurses.

Dana Gamble and Dr. Peter Hasler from the Public Health Department helped coordinate medical services, as did Sandra Copley, PHN, who oversaw a small army of nurses. Rape crisis and domestic violence counseling were made available. The FUND families provided care and incentive packages. Direct Relief International provided the leadership skills of Dr. Bill Morten-Smith and much needed medical supplies. Parish Nursing also provided nurses. What turned out to be the most important service of all was tuberculosis screening. Through the dedicated work and planning of many, a potential outbreak of this ancient disease was detected in time. We found that scores of people had been exposed, and some were in fact found to have active disease. All are either being treated or have been medically cleared. The Public Health Department is working vigilantly to contain what would otherwise have been a serious outbreak.

As a society that has allowed homelessness to fester and become institutionalized, we have played Russian roulette not only with our spiritual values but our physical well-being. In my capacity as a social worker for the homeless, I have seen third world sickness and infections run wild on the streets. Flesh-eating bacteria and MRSA honor no boundaries. Neither does tuberculosis. Project Healthy Neighbors was successful beyond my wildest dream—and nightmares. In conducting this mobile clinic, the biggest health event of the year, we were able to block a potential epidemic that may have not only taken lives but also cost a lot more to treat. Not only would the homeless have faced this potential deadly outbreak, but Santa Barbara as a whole would have also.

Throughout history, epidemics have cut across social lines without mercy. If, as a society, we no longer care about third world conditions and we allow the homeless to live as such, then perhaps we should care enough about our own health and those of our families to address this problem. And for a moment, we should honor the first responders, whose careers call them to place themselves between those infected and the rest of society. We are indebted to the people mentioned in this article, those who made the dream of Project Healthy Neighbors a reality.

Project Healthy Neighbors was a model for the local government collaborating with several outside agencies and the medical community, anticipating a problem and addressing it before it became a widespread menace. So the next time you cough and know it is nothing more than a cold, stop for a moment and think of the homeless, who constantly face third world diseases. And give thanks to the foresight and hard work of the professional medical community, who were successful this time in protecting us all. And give a thought as to how we will end homelessness—this national disgrace—before a truly horrifying epidemic comes roaring out of the streets to threaten us all. An ounce of prevention ...

The Magic that is Project Healthy Neighbors

Noozhawk.com, 11-26-08

They came in the early morning in twos and threes, sometimes alone. The soft shuffle of their well-worn shoes on the cold pavement was a musical tapestry to those of us who had arrived early to set up the tables and chairs and to keep chaos under control. Their warm smiles or distant, self-isolating gazes were our welcome. The mumblings of the mentally ill commingled with hearty "good morning"s and "thank you"s from others. These were the people that many of us had spent countless hours planning, securing supplies, raising money, and organizing for over the last year. The magic that is Project Healthy Neighbors, a mobile medical clinic for the homeless, was on full display on November 17, 18, and 19 at Casa Esperanza. One change from last year was an additional tent to house the new services provided this year. The coming together of our community to reach out to our less fortunate neighbors who find the streets home was truly inspiring. The doctors, nurses, and social workers plus the Casa staff and other providers and volunteers numbered well over a hundred; all reached out with respect and love to the homeless guests of the event. Nurses from DRI, County Public Health, Community Clinics, Parish Nursing, and Cottage Hospital staffed a series of stations and administered flu, pneumonia, and tetanus vaccines, among other medical services. Nurses Jan Fadden and Sandra Copley were everywhere those three days, dispensing professional services along with heart-warming smiles. The staff of Casa Esperanza was especially gracious in their hospitality. Free haircuts bolstered fragile egos, while professionals from CADA, the VA, the Housing Authority, Domestic Violence Solutions, the Department of Social Services, and others took care of a variety of vital needs, including HIV and tuberculosis tests.

This year, Soles 4 Souls provided hundreds of shoes, and, as always, the kind families of FUND ensured the success of Project Healthy Neighbor '08 with their hard work of providing the incentive backpacks that contained sweatshirts, rain ponchos, toiletries, socks, and, most touching of all, personal greeting cards from the children of FUND. To witness these families giving up a Sunday to bring this all together—especially the joyful yet hard work of the children—was moving.

We were able to add both women's health and dental care components this year. Besides the greatly appreciated and indispensable infusion of youthful energy from UCSB's Health Outreach, the crowning addition to this year's health fair were the students from Midland School. They not only assisted the homeless as guides but also helped with the distribution of shoes and, most important of all, showed the homeless that they mattered in someone's life; that as our neighbors, we cared.

Of course, the stars of the event were the four hundred fifty homeless men, women, and children who received these life-saving services and gifts. While many bent heads rest on heavy shoulders due to the harshest of blows of life, most offered grace, appreciation, and love to the providers that day. A wise man told me that spirituality was the inner connection that we all share with one another. For three days, that inner connection was on full display. Perhaps nowhere else is a project such as PHN possible. Here in Santa Barbara, in our little corner of the universe, the darkness that can be the human condition was pushed back, allowing the warmth of human love to replace it.

To put all this into perspective, the literal life and death issues that PHN '08 faced and attempted to overcome, we were notified of the deaths of four of our homeless neighbors during those three days. We also learned of the insidious continuation of the tuberculosis epidemic that is impacting so tragically the homeless community, one that has finally turned fatal.

Thank you to all who served throughout those days. I wish that I could name each one of you; yet I know it is unnecessary, as the homeless carry the gift of your concern, along with the picture of your kind and caring smiles, with them in their hearts.

Project Healthy Neighbors Serves Less Fortunate with Kindness

Noozhawk.com. 11-23-09

The man had a devastating stroke merely a week before, and now his world was restricted to a wheelchair. While his body was crippled, his dignity was intact, and he waited patiently. Another man was simply seeking an additional blanket to help ward off the cold when he sleeps on the uncaring streets. His advanced age multiplied his physical pain, which in turn intensified his humiliation over being homeless. The large woman sat uneasily in her wheelchair, also patiently waiting her turn—wondering how it had all turned out so wrong. Another woman was fortunate not to be physically crippled. Her injuries where were found inside her mind and spirit. I had seen her many times before, bruises painting her face with shame from numerous assaults. Yet the greatest heartbreak this year was the inclusion of children, never before seen.

Nevertheless, this day was going to be different for hundreds of other homeless people. For three days in November, the "least among us" became the first as they were treated at the largest mobile health fair for the homeless in the country. A small army of nurses from the county's Public Heath Department, Parish Nursing, and Cottage

Hospital, plus ordinary volunteers, were able to administer flu and H1N1 immunization vaccines, along with pneumonia and tetanus boosters. Medical professionals screened for tuberculosis and AIDS. Those in need of mental health services were offered help by the county's mental health services and New Beginnings Counseling Center. Veterans were screened and apprised of benefits owed them by the VA. Those afflicted with drug and alcohol dependencies were offered help by the substance abuse recovery team at Casa Esperanza and Project Recovery. Compassionate doctors organized by Dr. Lynne Jahnke were kept busy dealing with the mundane to the more serious life-threatening situations of our guests.

An equally impressive army of volunteers consisting of students from Westmont, clergy from local churches, members of Families United to Nurture Dreams (FUND) and concerned citizens offered help, dignity, and love to those who all too frequently go without. Students from Midland School helped the homeless find the right shoes, which were provided by Soles for Souls and a local donor. Direct Relief International and Public Health provided life-saving medicines. A philanthropy organization based in Los Angeles graciously and generously supported FUND, enabling them to buy hundreds of backpacks, sweaters, hats, socks, and other necessities of life for the homeless facing the harsh winter months ahead. The children of the FUND families, as in the past, personally hand-wrote heart-warming greeting cards with personal messages of support that each participant received.

As has been true for the past four years, Casa Esperanza was a gracious host and the staff were extremely helpful in making everyone feel welcome. Surf Media was instrumental in getting the word out about the mobile medical clinic.

The real stars of this event were the hundreds of homeless men, women, and children who faced a particularly cruel year, with twenty-six of their fellow travelers having died. Survival brings a sense of grace, and their gentle smiles, kind words, and appreciative expressions repaid all volunteers and professional staff with a commodity more precious than gold. For everyone involved, this life-affirming event spoke to the goodness of hundreds of people in our community who stood together: the housed and unhoused, the mentally ill and their professional helpers, the spiritually damaged and those blessed with faith, the sick and wounded and their medical helpers, the unemployed and those lucky enough to have a job during the "Great Recession": all came together as one community. For three days, the goodness of Santa Barbara was on display. During this time, we reached out beyond ourselves to our highest spiritual beliefs and saw our ideals become alive before our eyes.

I would like to personally thank the following people who worked with me over the last year in planning this service to the homeless: Dr. Lynne Jahnke, RN; Sandra Copley; Ralph Barbosa; RNs Jan Fadden and Jan Ingram; Imelda Loza; Merryl Brown; Ken Saxon; Martha and John Buttney; Reverend Teena Grant; Ben Munger; Will Graham; Rob and Haley from Midland School; and the ministers and others who saw a need during the event and jumped in with compassion and enthusiasm to ensure that PHN "09" went on without a hitch. And a special thanks to the local donors who wish to remain anonymous; without their help, PHN "09" would have been impossible.

By the Numbers
- *624 homeless people served*
- *400 H1N1 vaccines*
- *400 seasonal flu vaccines*
- *150 pneumonia vaccines*
- *75 HIV tests*
- *10 men and women placed in detox facilities*
- *400 pairs of shoes*
- *500 backpacks*
- *500 sweatshirts*
- *500 rain ponchos*
- *500 hats*
- *1,500 pairs of socks*
- *500 evaluations by outstanding doctors*
- *Spiritual connections that cannot be measured*

Book Four

The Spiritually Gifted:
The Mentally Ill Homeless

CHAPTER THIRTEEN

Women with Mental Illness

Noozhawk.com., 11-23-09

The mentally ill of our community face cruel cuts in services that will condemn many to the streets. Without the cooperation and full funding of the Mental Health Department and the community-based nonprofits, those in desperate need of shelter, medication, and help will be forced to go without. Before those damaged by this cruel disease face the streets, we need to look beyond the cold statistics to the very real people who make up those stats.

She was older than her age would indicate. Sitting motionless, mostly lost in a faded, overflowing granny dress, she played nervously with her brown hair, which was twisted with oil and dirt. Her face was colored a hard bronze by life on the streets. She struggled hard to control her speech, but her jet-driven, tangled thoughts spewed forth like an eruption of Mt. Saint Helens. She rocked the baby stroller while we talked. Looking down at it, her face was torn with concern. She wanted to know where she and the baby would sleep that night. And when would her doctor begin to prescribe chocolate baby formula?

Suddenly the noise and controlled chaos that percolated over from the shelter floor into the office receded. An uneasy quietness froze the room. I looked from the empty stroller into her eyes. Confusion was absent; only genuine concern for her phantom baby was there, as real to her as the pain that creased her lips. Gently I told her that the doctor would do what was best in this particular situation, but in the meantime she needed to focus on survival. Where would she stay, if not at the shelter? Where were her Social Security checks being mailed? She politely made an excuse about why she needed to leave, got up, and left. The last I saw her, she was wheeling the stroller and her phantom baby down the busy street. Would the sight of this disheveled homeless woman pushing a baby stroller turn heads? Or was she invisible, just another heart-wrenching sight to be avoided at all costs?

Phantom babies and phantom pregnancies are a common delusion among mentally ill homeless women. They look around and see other women of their age settling into expected roles of parenthood, with families. The realization burns deeply into their innermost thoughts, as does the knowledge that their illness, especially if left untreated, forbids them this passage. They have so much love to give and know all too well the ache of loneliness, of human disconnection, and their souls bleed when they look down life's road and see nobody looking back.

To the more refined, politically correct professional helpers, "Linda" was a sex worker. She described herself to me as a "hooker; a working girl." She was also a "strawberry," a woman who sometimes exchanged sex for drugs. I have seen a lot, heard even more, but when she told me that her going rate was five dollars a trick, a black cloud washed over me. I studied her closely when she told me about the relentless horror story that her life had been: of suicidal depression overwhelming her till it could only be held at bay by an infusion of street drugs; how addiction soon became the center, and then the bane, of her existence; and of her life on the streets and the johns who engaged her body and exploited her mental anguish under the pier. Even today when I close my eyes, I can still see their handiwork: her face colored a hodgepodge of bruised blues and dark purples, with black, dried blood frozen over hellish wounds. An inner voice within me cried out: How could anyone do this to another human being? How could anyone not see and feel the profound sadness that bled from her large, chocolate-colored eyes, the gut-wrenching pain that radiated out from her soul? How could anyone see anything other than a severely mentally ill woman who cried out for understanding, for human warmth and understanding?

"Kathy" brought me flowers once. Dirt fell from the roots of the plant that she had just pulled out of the ground. I gasped when I tried

to imagine the gardener discovering the empty hole in his carefully manicured garden. As gracefully as I could, I received the gift from her, dirt falling on my boots. She rushed off, late for a meeting with a rock star, the phantom father of her unborn baby: a gestation period that ran somewhere in the years, according to her ongoing story.

I found "Julie" in a shelter and eventually moved her into one of the low-income hotels, back when we had them. She was a short woman who carried her carbohydrate-heavy diet as excessive pounds that she hid under dresses self-sewn from discarded colored sheets. Once in the hotel she slipped into a reclusive life. She also made sad-faced dolls that hung from a string around her neck. Julie's mental illness trapped her inside herself, a lonely, desolate existence. The walls grew more impenetrable with the passage of time, until hardly a word was to be heard from her. She ignored the warnings about her habit of sitting on the window ledge of her fourth floor room with feet dangling out. Of course, the tragedy played itself out. One day she either fell or jumped, rushing to an end to her misery.

None of these women asked to be born mentally ill. Some would say that they are simply junkies, crazies, of no concern to the rest of us—that the homeless will always be with us. The problem is, I remember. I remember a time when this army of the night, the legions of homeless men, women, and children who haunt our streets, did not scar our moral conscience. During my professional career, initially I saw absolutely no women on the streets and very few mentally ill; now State Street is becoming an open-air asylum, with trash cans as cafeterias. Bushes, bus benches, alleyways, parks, and alcoves have become our new low-income hotels, and street drugs replace the psychotropic medicines that should take care of the terrors that haunt the deep canyons of these women's minds. I have seen the mentally ill homeless become invisible refugees from our undeclared war against those who act different from us, especially if they're poor.

As it is, there is not enough help. Cuts to the Mental Health Department will only add to these stories of the women who have each touched my soul. State Street will become even more often the cruel and final resting place for those damaged by the diseases of the mind. Is this really what we want?

Not only was this article published at noozhawk.com but also as part of an informational leaflet: In 2008 county Mental Health Services faced huge cutbacks, which would have been devastating to those on the streets suffering from mental illness. Emily Allen, an attorney for the poor, and I leafleted the opening night of the Santa Barbara Film Festival. We were quite the pair, standing at the red carpet entrance to the Arlington Theater as a soft mist fell, attempting to engage those attending, pleading for help in fighting the cutbacks. A great deal of community effort was organized around the cuts, fortunately with positive results, as the Board of Supervisors took a courageous stand and postponed the proposed rollbacks.

Reflections and Cutbacks

Noozhawk.com, 4-9-08

Now is the time for good people to speak out on behalf of those who can only speak within.

The Santa Barbara County Department of Alcohol, Drug, and Mental Health Services is proposing drastic cuts to those it serves. I can't help but see the faces of the troubled souls behind the cold statistics. And it's not like we already do such a great job housing and treating those condemned to the streets because of their mental illness ...

The early Saturday evening foot traffic on State Street was bustling. Tourists and locals were hustling for a good time, trying to leave the troubles of the world behind. The problem was that in the middle of all this hustle and bustle, trouble slept on a bench, huddled under her blanket. Days' worth of food crumbs lay scattered around her; empty water bottles stood like lonely sentinels besides her. Buried somewhere under all that rat bait were my business cards, the one she refused when I had tried to offer her help a few days earlier and the ones from the time before that and the time before that ...

With increasing despair, I had tried a variety of incentives to engage the wounded woman. Offers of a bed at a shelter, food, shower, and even cash were all turned down. During my brief conversations with her, she hid inside the blanket that was pulled tight around her, like an American shroud, reminding me of the burqa that imprisons women in Afghanistan. The difference is that over there, a politico-religious medieval system enslaves women. Here, the diseases of the mind do so. In both instances, terror is used as enforcement. Over there a terror-laden insurgency reinforces institutional hatred of women. Here, frightening mental delusions terrorize her daily existence, making her an internal refugee in her own city.

I tried to understand, to see from her perspective how the world— how Santa Barbara—must look. Her view is physically constricted to a narrow field of vision by the shroud, draped over her head and around her face. For her, life is lived within a tunnel. She keeps her head down, never to look another human being in the eye. Every person who passes her is a tool of her internal repressive system rather than a fellow human being to engage with, to share the joys and the sorrows of life.

I watched the citizens of Santa Barbara as they walked by. Many ignored her. I'm reasonably sure they didn't see her at all, so accustomed are they to bypassing in silence the homeless people who suffer from her disease. Others cut a quick glance to her and then quickly looked away, trying desperately not to let others catch them looking at her. Perhaps they fear that if they are caught staring at her she then becomes their problem. Or maybe it is to trick their conscience: if others don't hold them accountable, neither can their own internal sense of right and wrong.

But it was the third group of people that drew my interest that afternoon. The clenched jaws, the hard set to their mouths, the narrowed eyes identified them. They looked around expectantly, trying to catch the eyes of others. Their looks cried out for witness to this tragedy before them. They wanted others to share in the suffering of this poor woman. They are the good citizens who still open their hearts to those who live on our streets, in so much pain. They are the ones who question where all the tax monies go, if not to help someone like this. They are the ones who refuse to accept that paradise is only for the select few.

I looked closer at the woman on the bench, wondering if she felt the compassion and even love of these people. And once again I questioned and then cursed; why is it that the delusions and hallucinations of the mentally ill must always be so cruel? Since it's all make-believe anyhow, why can't it be of the gentle kind? I once had a client who saw colors with sounds. Gentle voices had soft, muted colors. The songs of birds came in vibrant colors.

But then reality came crashing back. A young man out with his girlfriend saw Bench Girl and threw her a hateful glare. He laughed harshly at her. Here I was, questioning the harshness of hallucinations, when the world we live in provides so much heartless cruelty. At least we can try to impact reality; the symptoms of the mind are beyond us.

I made a commitment to look up Bench Woman again, with a new incentive—as soon as I can think of one. I sucked up my courage and told myself to once again approach the powers that be to see if they would reach out to the troubled girl. I'll remember the young man with the cruel laugh, but I sternly told myself to remember all the good people who were troubled by the sight of this woman's plight.

It is the yin and yang of life: the good citizens of Santa Barbara alongside the bad. It's the age-old struggle for our soul, for what kind of people we are and just how much pain the homeless mentally ill must suffer before we step forward to end it. The answer is also the answer to what kind of people we are, what kind of community we have become, and who we strive to be.

On April 22, the Board of Supervisors will address the proposed ADMHS cuts. Citizens moved by the plight of the mentally ill men and women who will lose their housing and treatment options and end up sharing the bench with the woman of this article can use their democratic right to attend that meeting or call or write each supervisor. Now is the time to speak out.

My calling to work with the mentally ill at times took strange and humorous turns. For years I would either go into work early or stay late, after all of the other GR workers had gone home. I would then review their cases, looking for any clients with mental health problems. I would transfer those cases to me. The next morning, when the workers discovered their lightened caseloads, I told them I was merely averaging things out. Since they ended up with fewer cases, nothing was said, but enough strange looks were exchanged to re-sink the Titanic.

Alone She Sat

Noozhawk.com, 6-6-08

She used to sit at the Farmer's Market—quietly alone, her eyes cast down, lost to her inner world. Her face was drawn with overwhelming sadness. Her blonde hair hung in long dreadlocks. She would sit like that for hours, locked within the confines of her prison—whatever the label was for the disease of the mind that the psychiatrists hung on her. For her it was simple sadness, a force so pervasive as to cut her off from her fellow human beings, from anything that approached happiness.

Sometimes, when I had the opening and the fortitude to attempt a dialogue, I would be rewarded with her smile. Not only did the beautiful inner glow that came miraculously to life suddenly transform her face, but its radiance would lighten the immediate area around her. In wonder, I saw that everyone near her shared in her overwhelming sense of joy. I remember thinking, *What an incredible gift to possess, an awe-inspiring spiritual blessing.* I couldn't help but juxtapose this woman against certain men in the world, who bring so much pain and violence to others in pursuit of personal glory and empire building, while here sat this simple woman with such an incredible gift. Then came the other times, when she was hunkered too deep in the pain of sadness to acknowledge me, in an isolation so profound that it was like a brick wall encircled her.

The last time I saw her I bought her some fruit and a rose. Her smile was even more brilliant, more shimmering than usual as she received the gifts. She thanked me in a soft voice. I didn't see her again after that. Did she run because the simple act of buying her that flower threatened her? Did the voices warn her that kindness was a danger to her self? Or was confusion sown by the act? Of course, the alternatives—jail, the hospital, a dead body by the tracks or under some bush—were too painful for me to contemplate.

"Doug" used to push his shopping cart down the street. Because of his busted foot that refused to heal, the cart was more like his walker than the vehicle that contained his worldly belongings. We often talked about the curse of alcohol that had such a hold on him. At times he would struggle mightily against the curse, but when he

173

was alcohol-free, the voices and the sadness returned. Here was a choice to end all choices: the damnation of alcoholism and all that came with it, such as aloneness and homelessness, or sobriety and the door it opened to the terror of voices and crushing sadness.

Somehow Doug fought through and ended up clean and sober, on psych meds. The voices were contained, the sadness controlled but not eliminated. He was a brave and courageous man fighting overwhelming odds to a draw. I often wonder: would I have the same strength and courage?

Dr. J and I frequently went looking for "Ben." One would think an old man overcome with the disease of alcoholism and barely able to walk, even with the aid of his walker, wouldn't be much of a challenge to find, but he was. When we couldn't find him at his favorite trash can or bench, we would eventually run him down in the jail or hospital. It was hard to share this man's rapid downhill spiral to death, but that is the journey we chose to travel with Ben. When our offers of help are repeatedly turned down, the only alternative for us was to be there as part of the journey. We tried to lessen the suffering and the loneliness, to share the indignity of the streets with him and to help with his medical needs, to provide the old man with jackets, socks, sleeping bags, and companionship.

He shared the story of his children with us and bits and pieces of his life. We felt victorious when he smiled, the sweet, innocent smile of an old man passing to the other side. Someday, somewhere, his children will mourn when he dies, but hopefully they will know that their father had company and friendship on his final road trip, that people tried to lessen his burden and pain, that Santa Barbara was kind to this old man and that he got a measure of respect and honor, which we all deserve as we prepare to embark on our final journey.

These streets, our streets, are home to so many people. Many honor our city with their presence, with their gift of love and the care they give to others whom they perceive are even worse off than they are. Those of us in the caring professions and those kind citizens who find homelessness a national disgrace need to remember and honor those of our neighbors who find themselves homeless through life's circumstances. Someday all this will be behind us. Till then our friends on the streets need our help and our friendship, however we as citizens are moved to show it.

There are those on the streets who get inside your soul. Their pain and aloneness, the injustice of their disease and the circumstances of their daily lives tear at you, day in and day out.

Survival

Noozhawk.com, 3-3-09

Coming out from behind a dumpster, her home; she looks left and right, tense, making sure danger is not rapidly closing in on her. It's early morning, and the traffic is light. The menace she looks for is not violence, not yet; that comes later, when the sun falls. It is rather a danger that subconsciously gnaws at her; she has become the "other" to many, the cause of the economic downturn that has produced so much chaos and pain. Better than most, she knows the times are hard. After all, State Street is her home, a place she resides twenty-four/seven. She passes the empty storefronts and wonders why. It's hard for her to use her rational mind to process the screaming headlines of the newspapers telling of massive layoffs, skyrocketing unemployment rates, falling housing prices, obscene golden parachutes and outlandish rewards to businessmen who have run their companies and banks into the ground. Instead, her mind is controlled by a sickness that produces delusional and hallucinatory thought processes. When her mind is free of the terror of her disease, she must figure out where to eat and how to avoid getting hurt and being arrested. This is what she is searching for on the streets this morning.

A frown darkens her face. She has heard rumors of the homeless being murdered. She didn't know Ross Stiles, but he was a brother of the streets, thus her family. Neither did she know Gregory Ghan, but the same holds true for him. And then there are all the street beatings lately. She tries to be careful at night when she crawls behind the dumpster that offers her shelter from the prying eyes of others. Her frown carves deeper trenches into her face; she knows the dumpster offers no help should the haters of the night come looking for her:

the young men who pass her in the day uttering words of disgust and glances of contempt, always followed by mocking and cruel snickers. What would they do to her if they find her alone at night? A shudder shakes her. It's best not to think along those lines. Her mental illness offers up enough terror without adding reality to it.

Seeing no police, she begins her awkward gait, an offside stride. She's hobbled by the pain in her crippled knees and hurting back. She needs to hit the trash cans on State Street before last night's food is thrown away. Her lips pinch down; her heart aches from the conversations she has been hearing of late; some blame her for the economic downturn devastating the city. The words cut deep, for she would never hurt anyone intentionally—but still they blame her. They blame the homeless for driving the profits from the city. For the most part, she finds the beggars in Santa Barbara to be gentle, much more polite than the ones she is used to in the big cities. But she knows a few are rough—she also knows many of them are not homeless. That is the way of prejudice, projecting the wicked deeds of some from the larger community onto the defenseless few.

She guesses that is the way of the world, knowing that she and others, especially those with her mental disability, who look and act different than most, must take the blame. Does she wonder? Does it scare her, the penalty for that difference? Have Gregory and Ross already paid that price?

Survival is the name of the game for her. Nothing luxurious or glamorous. Nothing about treating her disability or securing her a future away from the cold and lonely streets. Basic survival, until society decides it's time for a change and offers her and others like her a helping hand and a welcome home. Till then, she must simply survive. She looks cautiously behind her. Did she hear her name being called? Did she hear the sound of running feet rapidly closing in on her? Will she survive until the promise of that better tomorrow?

Bench Woman Hides Behind Her Shroud

Noozhawk.com, 8-20-09

Being jostled by the tourist crowd, which is decked out in the loud clothes and boisterous voices that is Fiesta, takes me back a few months to another type of encounter. But there is also another player, one we ignore at our peril: Death hides in the shadows, his dark cloak pulled tightly about him. He ignored the homeless during July, raising false hopes that his speed-run through them had come to an end. Then his cruel mockery went on full display as his lethal embrace touched three more homeless people. The one thing they all shared in common was that they dared to be old—ancient, in fact, by his standards. Two men and one woman—all were in their fifties. One died in a shelter, another on the streets, and the last in a medical facility. All fell victim to his beckoning within a span of four days. Our indifference, such as to the young mentally ill woman above, who has so eluded his grasp, creates a gutsy game of chance, one with a terrible price.

Book Five

The Walking Wounded

CHAPTER FOURTEEN

One of the saddest parts of my job are the calls I get from parents looking for lost children, even though the "child" is often in their forties. These parents' hearts ache with unreturned love. Over the years, they may have caught brief glimpses of their children as they progressed down the slippery slopes of the purgatory of the homeless mentally ill. As often as not, the all too infrequent updates on the children they gave birth to come from cops, social workers, hospitals, and, tragically, the coroner.

When they first make contact, such parents will inevitably go into great detail about how they got my name. Next they'll try and assure me that they know all about the hopelessness of the homeless mentally ill and that they no longer expect miracles from professional strangers like me. I often get the impression they have been expertly dodged by many in the helping field, who grow tired of hopeless struggle. These parents have arrived at the unenviable position of simply wanting to know if their offspring is alive, knowing that "well" is a relative term, with little meaning in the context of an untreated disorder. The few times I can convince a mentally ill person to drop a parent a card in the mail or, hope against hope, to call home is testimony that miracles do happen, that they occur within the human heart.

And then there are the parents themselves; the elderly are particularly ill-equipped for the rough environment of the streets, especially when they are ill.

"Art"

Noozhwk.com, 8-9-08
    Coming back from vacation and rereading my journals, I ran across this article that I had written two years back about the sad death of an old man.

    "Art? What's wrong?" I asked, hoping against hope to keep my voice from cracking.

    "I don't feel so well. I hurt," the old man replied through chapped lips. I leaned closer to better understand. He had lost his false teeth somewhere along the line, and his speech slurred as a result. With mounting alarm, I noticed that his cheeks were hollow, like life was being sucked out of him.

    Art was in his bunk at the homeless shelter. I had gone upstairs with a nurse to check up on him. He needed to be in a hospital, a nursing home, or a hospice, not here or sleeping on the streets, where we found him.

    The night before, he had returned to us from the hospital. That evening, watching him wheel himself into the shelter in his wheelchair broke my heart. He looked worse than before his hospitalization. His skin color was off—a deadly ashen gray, a hue that I had come to know well over the last two years, when the homeless died at an increasing rate. It is the color of death—of skin deprived of oxygenated blood, of hope slowly crushed by poor nutrition, cold, and indifference. We had sent Art to the hospital five days earlier in a walker and by ambulance. He came back to us in a wheelchair, delivered by taxi.

    Upon his entrance to the shelter, I sat down with him and went through his few belongings. He had seven bottles of meds but no overall instructions of when or how to take them, at least none that I could find.

    With mounting frustration, a sigh escaped my own lips. I thought back to just last week. I found him on his hands and knees in the upstairs dorm. When I asked what he was doing, he replied, "Going to the bathroom." He was dragging his faltering body along on all fours, on hands and knees, while trying to hold his beltless pants up, his dignity dying along the way.

Rushing over, I helped him stand. Without his missing false teeth, his tongue protruded between swollen lips. I remember thinking it was the same way Michael Jordan used to play basketball. But this was no multimillionaire athlete. This was an old man dying in pain, alone and in despair, in a homeless shelter.

The "dumping" of the poor by jails, hospitals, and others to homeless shelters and the streets is, all of a sudden, newsworthy. But it has been a fact of life during most of my professional career. The so-called "safety net" was reduced years ago to a funnel that poured the neglected and poor into almshouses: homeless shelters. In these places, partially by design but mostly because good people answer the call in hurting times, a desperate attempt is made to connect with and help the new lepers of our age, those who are shunned by some and despised by others.

This soul-to-soul connection is often initiated by the homeless themselves, men and women who find the time and the need to reach out to offer help and hope to those without. Often, the poorly paid staff go beyond their job description to look out for those too sick to take care of themselves. And sometimes the outreach workers have the privilege of caring for their clients.

But all too often, it is not a feeling of privilege but pain that paints my world black. Two weeks ago, that morning I helped Art back into his bed, his moans slicing through the air, lacerating my heart; he pulled the blanket up tightly to his chin, leaving only his head sticking out. His eyes darted around in panic. His tongue stuck out. He reminded me of a child who thinks he can keep the night monsters at bay with a thin blanket. But Art's monsters came when the morning sunlight exposed harsh realities.

Art looked away. I could feel his embarrassment from the crushing knowledge that he was dying, dying in front of us, death before an audience of strangers.

"Art, everything is going to be all right. The ambulance will soon be here. They'll be taking you to the hospital."

"They don't want me."

Of course, what he meant was, "Nobody wants me. Nobody wants a poor, dying old man."

Art went back to the hospital that morning. He was returned to us and again readmitted back to the hospital. Thanks to the engaged heart and professionalism of a certain doctor (thanks, Dr. Bordofsky) and Sarah House, a sick old man was welcomed into a hospice, where he died within days of his last stay at a homeless shelter, surrounded by love.

His death cut deep. The images from his last two weeks on earth will stay with me for a long time. Who knows, maybe it is myself, years down the road, that I see, crawling in pain just to get to a bathroom, one shared by two hundred others. It's not a pretty way to go. Art will be missed. The manner of his death branded many of us to the core, mocking all of us, contemptuous of our spiritual beliefs, trashing our self-respect—where did it all go so wrong?

That was two years ago. So much has changed—so little has ...

A Cry for Help

Noozhawk.com, 1-6-09

Along with the cold winds and damp nights that usher in winter, a deadly stranger has made his presence felt among our homeless friends. He first surfaced last year during Project Healthy Neighbors III, when he was discovered hiding while he inflicted his damaging ways. This stranger has a long history of inflicting pain, suffering, and death—lots of death throughout human history. And of course he really isn't a stranger at all: tuberculosis has a sordid yet intimate relationship with us.

Most of us think of TB as a disease relegated to the Dark Ages, a nightmarish relic from the past. But it isn't. It finds a home with the vulnerable and weak, wherever immune systems are compromised. Think about it; who is more risk at than the homeless, our fellow citizens, who, paraphrasing President Roosevelt, are ill-clothed, ill-fed, and not housed? Bodies are made weak by constant exposure to the elements and the stresses of the streets. Bodily defense systems are weakened by worry about police sweeps, tickets, fines, and jail, plus the violent criminals who hunt them down like game. The homeless have not forgotten that Gregory Gahn's murderers still roam our streets, as do the thugs who find pleasure in rape and savage beatings.

When a person constantly worries where his or her next meal will come from, TB finds the open door. When a person looks at the calendar, hoping for December first so the extra one hundred beds that stay empty eight months of the year will become available to them at Casa Esperanza, TB finds an invitation. When a person tries to figure out which part of town is the safest place to be, TB finds a way in. Of course substance abuse sometimes plays a role, circumventing the miracle of the human body's defenses, just as untreated mental illness does.

Make no mistake about it, a quiet epidemic has ravaged our streets this last year. It broadcasts waves of fear when a new case is discovered. Whispers are exchanged, including the names of those hospitalized. The homeless wonder who will be the first to die from this disease. That guessing game is over, because TB has claimed his first fatality.

Since PHN last year, fifteen of our homeless friends have fallen victim. Public Health has responded, expanding their reach among the homeless in an attempt to get a handle on this epidemic. Public health nurses are in the vanguard, fighting valiantly in a desperate attempt to prevent what has just happened. When Dr. J and I conducted our mobile medical outreach that led up to Project Healthy Neighbors 08, we pleaded and begged the homeless to come in and take advantage of the wide range of medical services offered. We often stood and stared, deeply moved, into wounded eyes that showed so much sadness, resigned to their harsh circumstances. For far too many, TB is just one tool of death that hounds their every step. Hopelessness is tuberculosis's first weapon of choice.

But there are things that we can do as a community to help our friends battle this disease; as they fight it, they also fight our fight, for viruses and bacteria do not respect boundaries. If we are not morally moved about the national disgrace of homelessness, which we have allowed the politicians to ignore for too long, then maybe we should stop and think of the risks we expose everyone to by not doing so. We must be proactive in this fight or be prepared to pay a terrible price. We should question the wisdom of idling our first line of defense: the staff, doctors, and nurses of Public Health. Within a few weeks, the county's Public Health Department will sharply curtail services for two weeks. A worse time cannot be imaged. The phrase "penny-wise and pound-foolish" comes to mind.

If we can't find the means to immediately house those in desperate need of shelter, then perhaps we can make sure that come April 1, when the main shelter is forced to evict one hundred people onto the streets, that a special medical bay of thirty beds be established and funded. The injured and sick, the first victims of communicable diseases, should be allowed to find rest and shelter during their recuperation.

It has been pointed out that I risk feeding into the prejudice against the homeless; that some will use this knowledge against the very people I am trying so desperately to help. First, those inclined towards prejudice and fear of the homeless need no motivation; they will continue to let hatred rule their hearts. Second, the truth is the truth, regardless of whether it remains hidden or not. And finally, the homeless are endangered now. For the last year I have shared with the homeless the realization of what is transpiring. TB is here. We can ignore it and pretend otherwise, or we can try and do something about it. I am hopeful that the good citizens of our community will not react out of fear and prejudice but instead with compassion and will demand that more be done. I have offered two simple solutions. I'm sure there are many more, just as I am sure that the professionals of Public Health will continue their ethical duty in this matter. But make no mistake about it, more needs to be done, and done fast. In the meantime, as Dr. J and I conduct our medical rounds, we will search out the eyes of those we serve, knowing what might lie within.

A cardinal rule on the streets is never to turn your back on a drunk when you're breaking up a fight. Once a shelter staff member and I broke up a fight; the only damage that was inflicted was to the egos of the two falling-down-drunk combatants. Thinking I had the situation under control, I turned my back on the man I had a partial hold of. Of course, just as I did, he tried to lunge at the other man, but unfortunately I stood between the two of them. The three of us slammed into the side of the building, and one of the men stomped down hard on my foot.

Then there was the time a man went down hard in front of the shelter. He landed face down, breaking it open. Rushing over to aid him, I carefully tried to avoid the blood that ran freely down the street. Not seeing the paramedic who had come up behind me from the fire station across the street, I yelled for someone to go and hurry their "sorry asses." I also mentioned something about all the blood.

"That's not a lot of blood," the paramedic stated in disgust, his feelings obviously hurt by my words. *If it were your blood, it would be a lot*, I thought, but I managed to keep it to myself. I moved back, still trying hard to avoid the blood. By then, two paramedics had hooked the man up to a defibrillator device to try and shock his heart back to life. Suddenly I heard a strange, soulless voice cautioning one and all to step back. I looked at the two men, but when the warning was repeated, neither mouth moved. Then I realized that the voice was coming from the machine.

Another time, my future wife, then a outreach nurse to the homeless, was trying to help a homie who had had a seizure and fallen down in a soup kitchen. As she was bent over the man, a mentally ill paranoid woman began shouting that she was killing him. She yelled that the nurse was trying to inject him with poisons. I was pretty sure no one believed her and that nothing would happen, but it was the lunch hour; we were alone with scores upon scores of homies, many suffering from the same malady as the woman. What-ifs rained down on my own paranoia.

There was the time the LA Veterans Administration lost a Santa Barbara homeless vet who was sent down to their clinic for surgery, which they said was a matter of life and death. There was the time a homie was discharged to a homeless shelter from the hospital with a knife, gun ammo, and a replica of a gun in his backpack. And the time I found Kelly naked in a soiled sleeping bag, dying on a bandstand in a park, still registers as a walking nightmare whenever I stumble across that memory.

Bits and pieces of hundreds of lives gone bad swirl in my mind, like those annoying floaters that sometimes drift just in front of my vision. Images, clashing feelings, somber heartaches, and black humor are what are left at the end of the day. Sometimes in the early morning hours when the house is quiet, chaos speaks in a mournful wail in the dark zone between sleep and wakefulness. What was said, what should had been said, what should had been done, play and replay ad nauseam. It's the sandman's version of water boarding.

Failed Health Care

Noozhawk.com, 1-09

"Barry," a short, slightly built man in his early fifties, struggled to stand, but his damaged knees refused to hold him upright. He teetered and then swayed precariously, threatening to fall hard onto the unforgiving blacktop. Traffic was already stopped for him, and the last thing he needed was to take a header with an audience looking on. Panic warred with the pain that was already tattooed onto his face. I saw him quickly look back to his walker, useless at the curb. He had been given knee braces, but he had discovered they prevented him from standing when he was seated at the curb, and thus he had discarded them. Yet without them, even the walker couldn't prevent him from toppling over.

Cutting a quick glance left and right toward the stalled traffic, I hurried over to him with a wheelchair. I promptly grabbed him by the arm and as quickly as possible sat him down. Time became an enemy—the stopped traffic was unsure what to do. It was a testimony to the good people that none of them blew horns or cursed us. Instead, looks of compassion and sadness leaked from the cars, along with confusion.

My plan to rapidly expedite us away from the situation ran into the hard reality that Barry's legs didn't have the strength to lift his feet. If I pushed the wheelchair forward, they would become trapped under the chair and flip him onto the ground. But where there's a will, there's a way, so I turned the wheelchair around and instead pulled it backwards. Still his feet dragged along the ground. Dr. J rushed over, grabbed Barry's pants legs, and gently lifted them up, allowing greater speed for us and less pain for him. A moment later, success was achieved when we wheeled Barry into the homeless shelter. There was confusion as to whether he had a bed or not, and only after Dr. J and I pleaded our case to Imelda Loza, the assistant executive director of Casa Esperanza, was his placement secured.

It had been a hard day at the shelter. During the morning, I met with the kind and harried social workers at the shelter, David, Katie and Maureen, trying to get beds for an impossible flood of disabled and senior citizens who called the streets their safety net. Was the man with a deadly disease more in need of a shelter bed than the one crippled by a car accident? Or was the woman trapped in her wheelchair by a lifelong disability more in need of a bunk than the man who could hardly walk due to a stroke? Was the senior citizen supposed to sleep on the streets so a mentally ill homeless woman who thought terrorists were after her could get one night's sleep in the safety of the shelter? That was what the healthcare delivery system had come to: lifeboat ethics—who lives and who dies due to lack of resources, affordable housing, and shelter beds.

I flashed back to a few days earlier in the Community Kitchen, where I am privileged to serve lunch once a week. We have a custom of allowing the disabled to be served first. The first four people in line were in wheelchairs, the next four on crutches and canes; the ninth man walked with his blind stick held out in front of him. Then came women, seniors, and the disabled whose wounds are within: the legion of mentally ill who roam our streets.

I think fondly of "Nancy," a mentally ill homeless woman who Dr. J and I had been treating in the streets for weeks. Dr. Lynne Jahnke and I were running her down two to three times a week so her wounds could be cleansed and bandaged, and we knew that was all that stopped her from losing her leg. That knowledge propelled us along our weekly hunt through the bright city streets and dark back alleys.

Every one of these tragic tales speaks to a health care delivery system not only in crisis but in a state of failure. The stories speak to our communal denial of this tragic fact. Politicians debate whether healthcare is a right or a privilege in today's America. How about if we view it for what it is: a matter of life and death? Who among us can be certain that we are not the next Nancy? The next Barry? Or any of those unfortunate souls who, instead of homes and nursing facilities to care for them after catastrophic illnesses or injuries, find the streets or a shelter their recuperating station? Who among us is next?

CHAPTER FIFTEEN

Beyond Prejudice

Noozhawk.com, 3-15-09

"Michael" sat across from me, hip deep in the symptoms of his disease. Bloodshot eyes stared back, his speech was slurred, and the odor of stale booze hung around him like personal smog. I knew that he was an alcoholic, the kind of homeless person that many would label "bum." Some would even say that he and Santa Barbara would both be better off if he were dead. But then I think back to the drive to work this morning. As I was listening to my favorite country western station, the lyrics of the song "Feed Jake" caught my attention. It was about the "bums," sleeping on the city streets. It told how some don't care about them. But then strangely, especially in a so-called red neck song, the singer reminded us that their moms' do—and that he did. As I thought about it, the confusion lifted, for it became obvious that the singer's spiritual values dictated that he not judge; that as a moral man, he accepted that we are all less than perfect, and nobody is beyond redemption.

With that, a deeper knowledge was given to me, a hidden strength for looking beyond the superficial. I then dug into my memory banks for what I know about Michael. Before his disease drove him to the streets, he was a hard-working blue-color man. There was nothing glamorous about his work. He was the kind of man who built the wealth of our country, kept businesses clean and the economy functioning. Maybe pushing a broom and cleaning offices for years is neither sexy nor financially rewarding, but workers like him give all of us access to clean establishments and decent food in our restaurants. He also worked a lot with animals and paid the price with painful injuries.

A Christmas scene with him came to mind. I had tried giving him a gift, with the one proviso—that he not exchange it for booze. I asked him this based solely on his word of honor. Of course, most of us would take the gift and give false reassurances. After all, for many, honor is simply a five-letter word. Not for Michael. He gently gave me the gift back, saying his disease would force him to do the dishonorable thing. Honor was deeply ingrained in that man. For him, no matter how far down he had fallen, nobody and nothing could force him to betray it.

I think of another man suffering from alcoholism. Many pass him by daily, seeing only the long beard, the greasy hair; the unsteady gait. I have another vision of him. I imagine him as he looked in Vietnam—a brother Marine dodging the bullets, praying that the deadly mortars won't find him. I imagine him smelling the odor of rotten eggs while white phosphorous bombs hideously burn human flesh. I watch him watch the darkest of black and the brilliant red of a napalm strike, feeling the ground shaking and the folding of the air caused by the heavy concussions from a massive B-52 strike.

I also know that some will never know the terror of combat or its crippling legacy; some camouflage their cruel words and harsh judgments behind the anonymity of the Internet as they condemn this "fall-down drunk." I see a fallen hero, wounded in his own way, someone who paid the ultimate price, except in his case it is "death on the slow," delivered by a bottle. When he dies his name will not be on the Wall, but he and I know different.

I ask that we not demonize those we do not know. We can disagree on solutions. We can all reach our own conclusions about the problems of homelessness, but we are not entitled to our own set of facts. And we cannot judge a person till we get to know him or her, beyond our prejudices. When fear rules our hearts, tragedy inevitably follows.

The murderers of two homeless men, Gregory Ghan and Ross Stiles, still roam free. How much longer till justice? When were the last murders in our community that went unsolved?

Fear

Noozhawk.com, 6-3-09

I ask for your indulgence for one moment. I request that you close your eyes briefly and imagine that you are at home, alone, sitting and enjoying a quiet evening, minding your own business. Then imagine two scruffy homeless men entering your domain and accosting you. One of the two men grabs a blanket that you've been using—you stand and try to retrieve it. One of the two guys picks up a bottle and smashes it against your head, causing your brain to swell, resulting in your death.

Try to imagine another time; two or three homeless guys enter your house; again you are alone. They are upset with you. Maybe it's the way you dress, in nice clothes that are washed. Or maybe it's the way you smell of enticing perfume or sweet cologne. Who knows? It could be jealousy, or something that they thought you said or some obscure thing they think you stand for. Maybe they simply had a bad day, week, or month. For all these reasons, or no reasons at all, they attack you, cowardly and viciously, and beat you so badly that you die days later.

You don't live in a violence-wracked part of LA but in peaceful Montecito, Santa Barbara, or Goleta. Perhaps your dying thought is: Why me? The brutal homeless men didn't even know you, but they hated or feared you enough to kill you. Your last thoughts are of justice; at least the perpetrators will be brought to justice. Santa Barbara will care enough to see these thugs pay for what they did.

Now open your eyes. It's all just make-believe. You are safe; no one is hunting you. Unfortunately, for Ross Stiles it was all too real. Two guys did in fact enter his camp and try to take a sleeping bag. Can you imagine the pain he felt when the bottle shattered against his skull, the dull ache that slowly turned to excruciating pain as his brain swelled within the unforgiving confines of his skull?

What did Gregory Ghan feel when he was set upon by his killers? He was alone and defenseless. Feel the sheer terror he must have felt as fists and feet drove killer blows down upon him. Perhaps he also wondered how these kids, privileged enough to have apartments or *homes to go to at night, could find the hatred within their hearts to beat him so viciously, so cowardly.*

And if Alan was set upon while he sat in his wheelchair, what kind of courage did that take? He was a crippled man without a leg, fighting depression. And I don't even want to try and imagine the pain and helplessness Alex felt as his body burned. That is a pain that no one should endure.

Fear is one of the most terrible emotions that we possess. It makes us shun reason and see things that are not there. Sometimes when I'm at meetings and people begin to express their discomfort about being around homeless people, I close my eyes and imagine I am just a typical American sitting with a like-minded group of individuals any time in recent history. I can hear the talk about how encountering African American men at night frightens us—or dark-skinned Latinos, or swarthy Italians, or hot-tempered Irish Americans. You supply the racial stereotype, the "other."

But then I open my eyes and realize it's not really about them— the others, walking at night; it's us—our own fears, the fear of the unknown; especially of people different from ourselves. Maybe it's the mentally ill person who talks to him- or herself, or someone who smells different or perhaps dresses in dirty clothes. For sure it's fear of poor people who are forced to sleep on the streets. Maybe it's because their very existence challenges so many of our most cherished images of ourselves. Are we a compassionate people, striving to protect the weak? Or are we a predator nation that makes war on those different from us? Are we a nation of laws, with equality for all, regardless of our station in life? Or do we let multi-millionaire bankers desert sinking ships once their malfeasance has thrown millions out of work and depleted workers' hard-earned retirement accounts, while we accept freedom for killers in our community?

Obviously, I wouldn't bother to write about or attempt to share the knowledge of poverty and the injustices inflicted against the poor if I didn't know deep in my heart that the citizens of my community do care. I think that basically we are a good people—that we don't want murderers walking freely on our streets. Perhaps we may not always know what to do or how to effect change, but as a caring community, we must strive for justice for all of us. Ross and Gregory, and now perhaps Alan and Alex, wait for that justice. As a community, we dare not fail them.

Update

A kindly, frail veteran in his fifties is the sixteenth homeless person to die on our streets this year—sixteen. In all of last year, only eighteen homeless people died.

Fire Scars More Than the Victim

Noozhawk.com, 6-15-09

She held the paper firmly in her hands, afraid that otherwise it would tremble, betraying just how nervous she felt. At first her voice fought for control as she read from her notes. It was easier, she told us, to have written down her thoughts. She was usually nervous around people, she explained; besides, she worried that the subject matter at hand was too emotional. She feared that she would be overcome by it all. She also wanted to make sure she didn't forget anything, especially how kind Alex was—how gentle his heart. I'll call her "Linda." She is afraid that whoever had set Alex on fire, if that is what turns out to have happened, would come looking for her if her real name was used.

It soon became apparent that Linda was a naturally gifted writer. In her scribbled notes, the pathos of the cruel act of setting someone on fire contrasted sharply with the gentle, child-like faith she had in Alex. She related how he liked to please people, how he played guitar on State Street, to earn a little money but also to bring a smile to those of his community. She told us how he never had a harsh word for anyone but always a smile, always a kind thought and gesture. Now he lives in incredible pain, fighting daily for his life. I don't know the particulars of his medical treatment, but I know enough about severe burn wounds to know the general treatment. There will be searing pain as his burnt flesh is scrubbed away; countless blood transfusions; the pounding of intravenous antibiotics to ward off infections; skin grafts; and months, if not years, of painful rehab. And then finally, the psychological pain of PTSD as he relives the nightmare of being on fire. If this happened at the hands of another, as it appears, a more hideous crime would be hard to imagine.

But Linda's story was not about vengeance or necessarily pain and hopelessness. Instead, it was about a gentle man and a good-hearted woman. She told us how she had dressed up that morning and wore high heels. We smiled when she told us how difficult it was to walk through the ivy, her heals sinking into the soft soil. Then our smiles turned bitter when she told us of the terror that overtook her when she came upon his camp, only to find it fire-gutted. She called out his name, cautiously at first, and then in rising fear as panic overcame her.

Running away from the crime scene, she came upon a fireman on his morning jog. He told her that a homeless man had been severely burned in the shallow, cave-like camp. After others had refused him, the man had been transported to Los Angeles to end up in a burn unit in a hospital.

As a writer, I am always turning over different thoughts about what would make good fiction. Many ideas are rejected because who would believe them? Some are just too outlandish, too unbelievable. I remember thinking as I listened to Linda recite this horror story, This is my community; these types of hate crimes don't happen here. But then I remember Gregory Ghan, Ross Stiles, maybe Allen McGibben. And I think back to a young homeless man who had his throat cut in Alameda Park by college prep students out to do mayhem. I also remember an old man who was kicked to death across the street at Alice Keck Park by two youths. And then there was the murder of Linda Archer and Rose Doe—I never did find out her real name, just as I never found out who dumped her body at the Wilcox property all those years ago.

Maybe we're just better at ignoring the harsh truths—the darkness that patrols our streets and some of our hearts. After all, we are similar to many communities where hate crimes against the poor do take place.

But then I look at Linda, and this kind woman with a gentle disposition and tremendous compassion reminds me of the good in our community, which stands in such stark contrast to the bad. For as surely as evil walks among us, so does goodness. It's just that at times it's hard to remember that; we seem to be so good at turning our backs on unpleasant truths. But the funny thing about truth is that it exists, regardless of how we spin it or how we ignore it. Getting up to leave, I remind myself that the job at hand is to align our moral beliefs with the truth. The truth may not be what we want it to be, but our struggle is like the Civil Rights workers in their day: to bring reality in alignment with our moral beliefs. Our fight is different in a way, but, then again, not so much. Evil must be confronted before it can be overcome. We owe Alex and the others no less.

Driving along 101 just past the Haley St. onramp, I can see the remains of Alex's camp. You can see the burnt brush that hid such a terrible crime. And, in the quiet of the early morning, you can hear his cry of pain alongside the screams of injustice.

Update

"Dave" was the seventeenth homeless person to die since January. He lived in a park and worked at the harbor. His whispery beard highlighted his youth and innocence. He was a good kid and will be missed. We are one death away from a cruel marker. Eighteen homeless deaths were recorded during all of 2008

Twenty-Fifth Homeless Death and a Woman's Story

Noozhawk.com, 10-2-09

Even though it happened several months ago, this story still lives with me every day. It had been a brutally dry winter; every forecasted rain event was a no-show. Perhaps that was why the late storm that actually delivered rain jacked the emotional level of the shelter toward a manic meltdown. The shelter was crowded with all sorts of homeless: those seeking escape from the elements, as well as those trying to elude the terrors of their minds, be it mental illness, the scourges of alcohol and drugs, or plain, simple despair.

I had started my rounds earlier that morning on State Street, looking for a homeless woman in need of medications. The gutters were running fast and deep from a downpour, and unable to negotiate a leap, I had landed in the middle, soaking my shoes and socks. With sarcastic humor, I looked up, thinking this was not the way to start the morning. It was an omen of a bad day. If I had only known.

Back at the shelter, I tried to cut my way through the crowd of soaked bodies, fielding questions and requests left and right. Bed extensions were needed by some to prevent them from sleeping in the rain. Others needed to see a doctor, or a referral to Social Services, or a thousand and one other needs that come with being at a homeless shelter. When "Susanne" saw me, she stood up. As is her pattern, her eyes were flighty, darting up to register a greeting and then retreating. "I've been waiting for you," I heard her say as another voice from behind asked for bed rest.

I was in a hurry and impossibly rushed, so I told the second person to come with me to the doctor's station and planned to tell Susanne I'd see her later in the day. But a darker pain than usual shadowed her darting eyes and brought me to a quick stop.

"I need to talk to you," she stated, slowly but firmly.

"Okay," I replied.

"Not here. In private."

I really didn't have the time, and I knew that her mental illness frequently forced her into rambling, pressured, and time-consuming one-sided dialogues that tested my patience. But something was off—something tragic was forcing her hand, and now mine.

"Okay. Come with me," I told both women.

Once in the doctor's office, I quickly took care of the bed rest request and ushered that woman out the door. Turning to Susanne, I smiled and asked what I could do for her.

"I was raped."

The three quietly spoken words, terrorizing words, shattered the normalcy of the morning. I tried very hard not to look toward the doctor, Lynne Jahnke. I wanted to focus on Susanne, and I wanted her to know she now had my complete and undivided attention. I quickly shut the door and sat down next to her, my hand on her shoulder, trying to comfort her. Hers was a story straight from hell. Multiple rapes had occurred over time and distance, increasing her shame and pain; she was further humiliated when she saw others witness it and do nothing to stop it.

I quickly decided to take her to the hospital. Walking through the shelter to get my car, my mind reeled. I remember trying to cool down homeless men who threatened retaliation against the perps, telling them the police would take care of it; and of comforting homeless women who milled about in shock and fear as the rumor mills cranked into high gear over Susanne's assault.

On our way to the hospital, I gently tried to ascertain exactly what had happened. Once there, we were put into a small room with dimmed lights as we waited for the police and the sexual assault team. For an hour, the details of the horror became a stream of consciousness from a damaged mind. I shuddered when she told me of the beatings and torture her husband had subjected her to; of trying to raise and protect her children in that hellhole, and how she slowly lost her grip on sanity—and now this.

How could one person be made to bear so much? I could hear her fractured soul reeling from a lifetime of pain: she was a battered wife, a homeless woman, a rape survivor. But strength was present as well. She refused to allow neither the rapists nor her husband to steal her soul. She told me she knew that she was a good person, a person of God, and that her deity stood with her, as did the doctor and I.

Walking out of the ER, out of the nightmare, I found that the weather had cleared. It was brisk and life-affirming. Looking up, I saw that the purple mountains had been dusted with pristine snow. Contrasts between the grace of nature and the dark heart of mankind clashed. I cast a quick glance over my shoulder, looking for and thinking of the penalty that is imposed upon the mentally ill and the cruel consequences of either being born that way or broken by life's experiences. And I asked the silence, "Has God simply walked away from a world lost in violence and hatred? Has God forsaken us as we have forsaken those afflicted with mental illness or subjected to unspeakable violence?" Do we have a right to ask God not to if we continue to do so?

Postscript

"Larry," a talented artist, becomes the twenty-fifth homeless person to die this year. This "transient" was born and raised here and lived his entire adult life in our community. In the end he was

broken by the fastballs and sliders that life hurled his way; Oak Park was his final home. This man was talented beyond belief—such a tragic waste.

Memories of Good Friends Live On

Noozhawk.com, 10-21-09
    I finally discovered what "Charles" did with that large suitcase he was never without. For years he sat on the same bench, watching time flow by like the traffic does on his part of State Street. It was like he was waiting for something, always watching. I wasn't even sure that he knew who I was, till one morning he said, "Hello, Ken." It was an acknowledgement, a breakthrough of sorts, but he still refused help. And for years that large suitcase would sit next to him, his faithful companion. I assumed it contained all his personal belongs, including a ton of clothes; he was always neatly dressed and well groomed. He was a small man, advanced in years and on the frail side, so whatever was in the suitcase couldn't weigh much.

    I remember one time when I found a homeless woman who needed a bandage change for her leg. There were no empty benches around. I told her we could walk down to the next block. Charles snapped out of the cold distance existence that he lived and told me we could use "his bench," the one he was sitting on. I was deeply honored. It was like someone offering me the use of his or her house. I watched him grab his suitcase and walk down the street.

    Weeks later, at 7:30 in the morning, I had stopped to get my morning fix of caffeine. The streets were deserted and quiet. I walked past a storefront and looked in and saw Charles. He was asleep, curled up inside his suitcase. He had unzipped it, folded it out, and presto: instant bed. A pillow and a few items of clothes were all that the suitcase contained. Not exactly the secure retirement most of us plan for.

    "Doug" is a kind and gentle man. He plays music for the benefit of others. I've never had the courage to ask him if he actually hears sounds from the make-believe musical instruments that he plays so passionately. I firmly believe people are entitled to their delusions. Before now, in a more innocent time, we called them eccentricities.

Doug often suffers from debilitating bouts of depression—so deep that it brings tears to my eyes and searing pain to my soul when I can't figure out the magical words to help him break the bleak mood. For such a good-hearted man to be so punished makes me realize the extreme depths and cruelty of mental illness. But there is always the stark contrast of the magical music he shares with the world in his attempt to bring cheer to others.

For months Dr. J and I have gone weekly to clean and bandage the series of life-threatening wounds of a mentally ill woman. She too always turns down our offers of help, of placement in a shelter or hotel. In fact, she has always paid for our services. Every time we finish taking care of her wounds, she hands me a handful of diamonds as payments. To some they are nothing more than broken pieces of safety glass. To me, more brilliant diamonds would be impossible to imagine. This woman has made me a wealthy man, beyond my wildest dreams.

There is the homeless man I meet almost every morning as he makes his way from morning services at the church that he attends to the soup kitchen. He told me how his life shattered years before, when he had suffered a massive heart attack and was technically dead for eight minutes. In a soft, confessional tone he shared with me how, during those dead minutes, he traveled to heaven before coming back to earth. Who among us wouldn't have their life altered after such an event?

I had dealings with another man who also deeply impressed me. He told me how he had spent the money when he received a lump sum payment after an industrial accident. He had given some of it to a friend of his who had just lost her job. She was a single mother with two kids who happened to have one great and kind-hearted friend.

Then there was the man, a hard worker all his life, who found himself sinking into homelessness when the hurricane of the recession hurled itself upon our land. The overwhelming despair he felt ended when he shot himself.

For some reason, the memories of these good friends accompanied me this morning as I walked down a deserted street. I think maybe it's because death was held at bay this one week, allowing me to contemplate the humanity of those who tragically call these streets *home. They aren't bad people—in fact, some are near saints in their compassion for others. Many are damaged by life's circumstances beyond their control. They are our neighbors, asking nothing more than to be greeted with a warm smile and a gentle hello: the same thing each one of us would welcome, especially if we were sick and downcast. Small gestures can often carry so much meaning and so much kindness, and the cost and effort are so very little.*

Update

Unfortunately, Death's reprieve was all too short; John E., homeless, age seventy-one, a long-term member of our community, died in jail. He was the twenty-sixth homeless person to die this year, the ninth elderly man in his seventies since the Memorial for the homeless dead this summer.

The Numbers Can Be Overwhelming, but Help Is Here

Noozhawk.com, 1-13-10

The air was cold, and I was bundled up in my leather jacket, unlike the young man who stood before me. He was wearing a woman's coat that may have been fashionable at one time but was definitely not built for foul weather. Our breath was visible in the early morning air as we stood and talked. He also carried an overflowing black plastic bag, filled with whatever worldly possessions he owned. He was respectful, shy in fact, and clearly mentally ill. He refused my gift for him at first, until I reassured him several times that he was of course able to use it as he saw fit. When I tried to broach the idea of a shelter or the warming center, he withdrew into his armor of mental illness, reacting like a hunted deer.

Because of the kindness of a few people from Santa Barbara, I had embarked on the heartbreaking yet inspirational journey that led me to this encounter. One friend of mine, having read about the harsh conditions on the streets during the cold snap, ordered hundreds of pairs of gloves and rain ponchos. Another, a hidden saint of our community, when asked by his equally saintly wife and children what he wanted for his birthday, said a shopping trip for the homeless at a sports store. Within moments, goods flew off the retail shelves;

this man's concern for our friends on the streets became concrete. And more help came from others in our community. So I was armed with much needed supplies when I hit the streets looking for those in need. I decided to keep notes about who received their unnamed benefactors' help, mindful of some of the responses to my articles: my attempts to humanize those who call the streets home.

Out of the first twenty recipients, ten were clearly mentally ill, showing classic signs of schizophrenia, bipolar disorder, and/or severe depression. One person I was uncertain about, as he wouldn't engage in meaningful conversation. Three were severally physically disabled, two in wheelchairs, one a deaf-mute. These first statistics generally applied during the rest of my special project.

At the end of the day, sitting at home and reading my notes about who I had served, I was sadly shocked. I should know better—after all, I live in that world, day in and day out. That 50 percent of the first twenty were in need of mental health services says a lot. I would suggest that when people ask what can be done, or when others imply that the homeless are just people making a lifestyle choice, that we remember this statistic. If instead of seeing the homeless as stereotypes, we need to break down this generic catchall into specific categories and see them first as individuals and then ascertain what their unmet needs are. Based on my experiences I would conservatively estimate the composition of the homeless to be as follows: 35 percent mentally ill; 20 percent families and children; 25 percent the physically disabled, the fastest growing subgroup of homeless; 20 percent are veterans according to most studies; 30 percent are those afflicted by the curse of addiction. Of course there is overlap, but the point I would like to make is that the tragedy of homelessness can only be resolved when we move away from fear-induced stereotypes and address the reality before us. This also offers a way out for those who find some of the behaviors of those who find the streets home objectionable.

None of us can save the universe, but we can address the needs of those on our own streets and come up with solutions according to what moves our own hearts. If one finds it scandalous that a combat veteran should return home only to become homeless, then please make the Veteran's Administration finally fulfill its moral contract. If homeless children stir your heart, then make the politicians put our children's needs first. Our community can make a great difference if we move away from stereotypes to reality by reaching out a helping hand to one person at a time.

Another frequent response to my articles comes to mind. Many have asked what they can personally do. With my friends as examples, it's clear that our community is blessed with many caring and compassionate people and organizations. For those interested in homeless children, Transition House is a godsend, as is the Mental Health Association for the mentally ill. They are one of the finest organizations I have been fortunate to work with. While some may find a measure of fault with the Salvation Army and the Rescue Mission, we must respect the literally hundreds of lives saved by them. The Rape Crisis Center and Domestic Violence Solutions are still greatly needed by many, and both do outstanding work. Casa Esperanza is moving toward utilizing volunteers. The Organic Soup Kitchen, Consumer Action Coalition, and Jeff Shaffer's efforts to feed the poor are other examples of local solutions.

Returning to my friends, who insist on remaining anonymous but who have done so much good over the years: your efforts lead to only one conclusion—angels do in fact walk among us, and we are much richer for this. I would like to thank each one of you on behalf of those whose lives you have touched and, in fact, helped save. You have also uplifted me many times when despair has threatened to overwhelm me.

A Sad Update

Greg, a good friend of mine who happens to be homeless, died on 1-8-10 at the pier. He was fifty-three years old.

The Story of Two Women: *"Kathy"*

Noozhawk.com, 2-18-10
(Note: this is the first part of a two-part article)
"Kathy" and "Danny" are two women of the streets with radically different outcomes. Kathy's story illustrates that lives can and are saved when lifelines are there for them, even against all rational

odds. These desperate lives can have tragic outcomes without a helping hand in a moment of crisis.

Pain leaked from Kathy's pale blue eyes, despite her best efforts to hide it. Her blonde hair softly framed her face, cushioning the hurt that leached out from her. Everything moved slowly—awkwardly. The quiet early morning, having robbed the streets of sound, intensified the emotions of this fragile woman. I was tense at first, sensing the wounded soul who sat across from me. But then I caught myself. She was anything but fragile. This was a courageous woman, one who had been through hell and emerged stronger for the struggle.

I looked closer, seeking the woman I used to know. For more years than I care to count I would steel myself when visiting the homeless camps, afraid of finding Kathy's body. She was always at the top of my list of those I feared would have died over the night. For years, this woman was driven to drugs and alcohol by a hellish life and the terrors of the symptoms of her mental illness, as well as by emotional scars that tore at her soul and had propelled her to the streets in the first place. I also feared that she would fall victim to the sick men who hunted vulnerable street women. Or that she would hurt herself to quiet the raging voices and psychological wounds. Or that she would simply go to sleep, never to wake up.

In her days on the streets she would provoke deep emotional pain within me whenever I ran into her and was unable to convince her to abandon the streets and come into the shelter system. I knew that in some ways the shelters are pretty bad choices for her needs, but I also recognized how much worse the viciousness of the streets can be for the mentally ill and women, the elderly, veterans, people who are sick or wounded, displaced workers. I deeply wish that there was an alternative, but there isn't. The government and society had taken away all other options for people like her.

Incredibly, over time she found courage, a great deal of it, and fought through everything that was thrown at her. With the help of the Rescue Mission and others who never gave up on her, she fought through the hell that was her life.

Looking across at her now, again I had to struggle to remember the wounded, and, in a very real sense, hunted, woman that she used to be. I sat back, thinking how much courage she has had to have to arrive where she was this morning. It would have been so simple for her to give up, to end her live in a haze of numbing drugs and alcohol. But she didn't. She endured the painful withdrawal from that life of drugs and alcohol. She didn't vanquish the demons that had driven her to the streets in the first place, but she did manage to fight them to a standstill. A fight that I can see in her troubled eyes is still a daily struggle for her.

A more courageous person I have never been privileged to know. Again, for the hundredth time, she and others like her show me that no person is without hope. Even the hard-core alcoholic or drug addict can struggle back. The survivors are so much stronger than me, having fought through a hellish existence that I can only begin to imagine. They have so much to teach me, to teach all of us.

I'm proud to call Kathy my friend. I am humbled by her life journey, her struggles, pains, and triumphs. This remarkable woman has been clean and sober for over two and one half years. She has reconnected with family and with trepidation and courage faces a life free from the slavery of addiction. Thank you, Kathy, a friend I deeply honor and respect—in fact stand in awe of.

The Story of Two Women: "Danny"

Noozhawk.com, 3-7-10

(Note: This is the second part of a two-part story: The Story of Two Women)

A nightmarish consequence: What happens to those who are turned away from a shelter when it shrinks from two hundred beds to one hundred? "Danny"'s journey was in some ways different from that of so many other homeless and yet all too familiar. She had repeated the by now all too common journey for far too many years. She suffered from the ravages of mental illness, along with more than a hint of a substance problem. She, like many women, was chased from secured lodging by domestic violence. She did what she always did when the brutal man came after her—she ran. She was desperate to put distance between herself and the destructive forces overwhelming her life. In plain English, she was looking for sanctuary—for a helping hand and understanding, no different from what most of us would want in our moment of need.

Sadly, her journey took a tragic turn when she sought help—a calm bay to shelter her from the churning waters of the storm threatening to overwhelm her. She ran to Santa Barbara as she had in the past, but times were different, harsher, and the shelters last spring and summer were full. She secured an emergency bed for the night, but the city was at war with its homeless; resources were scarce, beds tightly controlled, and many perceived a vagabond, a transient, as not one of our own and, in some absurd way, the reason for our economic downturn. (I guess the banks and Wall Street get a pass.) I wonder how she saw herself, and if one believes in God, if he saw her that way?

I anticipate that some will fault me because I'm championing a foreigner in our community, but in truth I do not see her as a transient. I see a woman in a desperate search for help, for a life free from the torments of the mentally ill and the terror of domestic violence. A human being trapped in her aloneness, not knowing where to turn for help—when she did, the inn was full.

When we restrict beds at the shelters during the worst economic downturn in eighty years, who lives and who dies quickly boils down to lifeboat ethics. We put shelters in the cruel situation of trying to save the most vulnerable, but we aren't God, and we don't have the resources that are needed. The staff at the various shelters do an incredible, and in many ways heroic, job with very limited tools. The staff of each shelter and the outreach workers must look into the eyes of the homeless and send some—too many—back to the streets, back into the violence and the cold and the terror of the unknown. And we send some back to the terror of the known, back to the drug dealers who prey upon the weak and the vicious men with hardened fists who do so much damage to body and soul.

I look at the picture of Danny that I hold; there's no denying the pain in her dark eyes. Her brown hair falls softly to her shoulders. She holds her head tight and defiant, slightly upward, expecting— preparing for—the next blows to be delivered.

In the end she retreated back from where she came—back to her death. Within days came the call from the police, trying to retrace the footsteps of the last days of her life. Life is a little sadder knowing that we were unable to help this woman when she attempted to escape her fate. And I have an uncomfortable, sinking feeling—what would it feel like if I should stumble and need that helping hand? Will it be there for me?

I don't have all the answers to problems of limited resources and bad state governance that wastes hardworking taxpayer's money, or how to fix the severest recession since the 1930s or a dysfunctional mental health delivery system. But I do know that in the end the labels that we put on one another to shut ourselves off from each other diminish us all. "Transient" is such a word.

Danny was a woman in need of our help, and I'm sure most would want to help her in some way. She was a wounded woman who found no place to escape the pain. I hope she has now finally found the peace that so cruelly eluded her in this life. Danny was all of forty-three years old.

Do not go gentle into that good night.
Rage, rage against the dying of the light.

Dylan Thomas

CONCLUSION

Does God play a role in all of this? How could God sit in heaven and ignore all this suffering? These questions pound away at me constantly. As with Vietnam, there have been many heated discussions between God and me on these subjects. Inevitably the arguments come back to a couple of stories.

A deeply religious man took a cruise. While strolling on deck, he was thrown overboard by rough waters. Because he believed so deeply, he calmed himself by praying that God would come to his rescue. A merchant ship came along and offered to take him aboard. He turned the offer down, knowing that God would come to his rescue. The ship passed him by, and within hours the man drowned.

Arriving in heaven he found God waiting for him, a very angry God. Immediately the man became defensive, questioning God why he had not come to his aid. After all, he was a believer. God replied, "Who do you think sent the ship? And why do you use your belief in my existence to do nothing?"

Maybe that's the whole point. Either God or nature gave us intellect and compassion, as well as the resources to bring an end to homelessness, to refrain from engaging in war. We have the tools and the wherewithal. We also have free will—as the existentialists like to remind us, we are "condemned to be free." All we need is the willpower. We have neither excuses nor anybody to blame but ourselves. It's up to us to not only climb aboard the rescue ship but also to help those in need up the ladder. We can't look outside of ourselves for the answer. It resides within each of us. The answer, or lack thereof, defines who we are and what we are, and we cannot shift the blame elsewhere. We either demand that our society and our government bring the national shame of homelessness to an end or we accept the responsibility that we allowed this sore to grow and fester till it blights our nation and all of us, citizens and neighbors.

In the meantime, the casualties continue to mount. The streets, my streets, are lonely when I walk them now. So many friends have died. Santa Barbara is a different place without them. Cathleen, Pushcart Greg, Randy, Doc, Cobblestone, Stony Tony, Red, and so many, many more are gone. I catch myself looking for them in their old haunts: a park, Haley Street, the beach, in nooks and crannies known only to them and me—hideaway homes for those without houses. I find myself listening for sounds that exist no longer: the gentle strumming of a guitar, soft laughter from deep in a park, the clanging of a broken shopping cart—the symphony sounds of the joys and pains of life, forever stilled. The streets are lonely without you. I miss you all.

I look back, refusing to forget how the city's disregard for the poor allowed city government to do nothing while hundreds upon hundreds of beds in low-rent hotels were lost so new, exclusive hotels and time-share condos for wealthy out-of-towners could be built. More beds were lost than all the homeless shelters combined can offer.

You only have to see the boarded-up California Hotel on lower State Street and the vast hole across the way to understand how money talks. Rules are bent and deadlines extended for those with wealth and power while the poor die without shelter and this beautiful hotel stands unused. For five long years it's been that way. I know that eventually she will come down and with redevelopment the high-end condos will come along, but they cannot replace the memories of those who died here. The streets are a blank slate that we write on each day.

But I also acknowledge the unsung heroes who try to balance the scales of justice. Cindy, my haircutter, forgoes her fee, asking me instead to take the money to the streets and use it as needed. The father of my son's friend taught homeless kids how to play golf. I praise the kind church people who staff the soup kitchen and cook the meals at Transition House and the generous people who provide financial support to all the homeless shelters and programs. And I honor my anonymous financial backers, who have done so much to balance the scales of justice and have brought relief from the pain of the streets.

In the Jewish belief and other religions, there are angels among us, sent down to try to balance the scales of injustice, erase the pain of poverty. These angels, examples of what we can aspire to, also keep me going as I strive to walk in their steps. And sometimes angels live on the streets.

The Gift

Unpublished

An early Monday morning was greeted by a weak sun. My thoughts were on the nice weekend that I had spent with my wife and son, so at first I didn't notice "Cheryl" standing in front of the hotel. When my mind finally accepted the cruel reality that the first day of the workweek had begun for working folks, I noticed her staring at me. Her eyes were guarded, as if she were hiding a troubling secret.

"Morning," I offered cautiously.

"You know "Cathy," blonde, staying over at the shelter?"

The strain in her voice brought me to a halt.

"She died Friday," she offered in a hushed voice.

Cathy was a woman I had known for over twenty years. That is more years than I have known most of my friends. I saw her struggle greatly against the sadness that chased her into a troubled life. I have a hard time recognizing her as the embodiment of evil, as some do. All I know is that she was a sweet, caring woman who fought hard against the demons that chase far too many homeless men, women, and children to an early grave. I always knew when she was headed for a break by how much energy she put into her work. She was the type of worker who poured her soul and all her strength into whatever job she had. Whenever her workweek veered towards sixty hours, the crash was not far behind. And now she was gone.

I listened to a story about another woman, whose only crime was to be poor and mentally ill. She told me how the feds had denied her disability benefits. She received the news while locked in a psychiatric facility while recovering from a suicide attempt, not her first. In disbelief, her voice weak with pain, she told me how the medicines that would help the most were beyond her financial reach. I listened to that horror story while tears washed down her face—liquid despair.

I think back to last week at the shelter. We had sent "Bob" to the ER four times; and three times he was sent back to us. He vegetated for weeks in his wheelchair at the shelter, waiting either for fate to show him the way off the streets or to die; he was too sick, too tired to offer much of a struggle on his own behalf. The morning I sent him back to the hospital, he almost fell twice when he attempted to stand while waiting for the paramedics. The poor man's legs were hideously swollen and infected, bright red, weeping fluids. How could this old man have been discarded, sent back to the shelter and the streets in his condition? Was it a sick cosmic joke or the cruel punishment we inflict on the mentally ill and poor?

The shelter's logbook quoted a paramedic asking, "When did the shelter turn into a hospice?" He was alluding to the great number of dying people who were living out the pitifully few remaining days of their lives in, of all places, a homeless shelter. Talking to the Sarah House manager last night, she thanked me for sending them four homeless people over the last few months. She also felt bad about the one referral that had gotten away, a wheelchair-bound woman who died at Casa Esperanza before the needed paperwork could be completed. Of the four referrals, three had already died.

"Doug" came up to me. When sober, he had vague recollections of doctors talking to him about cancer. When under the influence, his cancer was the farthest thing from his mind. Today, the booze won out, and he waved off my concern for his health.

"Has he been drinking?" I asked his girlfriend the obvious question.

With a roll of her eyes, she acknowledged the stupidity of the question. Her eyes became hard and small, as she thought of life without her companion, thought about her own severe physical condition, one that threatens to render her a cripple.

Walking down State Street, I think of all the heartache that the homeless are forced to live with. But then the graciousness of the streets approaches me.

"I have something for you," the homeless woman tells me. I look down at her arthritic, crippled legs, noticing the layers of clothes that encase her worn body. Slowly and with delicate precision, as if she were unwrapping the most precious gift in the world, she peeled back the layers of tissue that she holds within her clenched hand. Reaching a large nugget of broken glass, she frees it from the tissue and smiles, not something that she does frequently.

"It's a diamond. You can have it cut and polished, put it in a ring."

"Thank you," I replied when she placed the broken glass in my hand.

"Praise God. I was looking for you." Her smile broadens. It is without doubt the warmest smile I have ever seen. Her face is beautiful, and the smile erases years from her advanced age. Then her eyes cloud over, her face becomes pinched, and she shuffles away, the pain in her legs obvious. Yet I knew that God gave her a bigger heart to compensate for whatever her illness of the mind may have robbed from her.

I continue my journey, now balancing the heartaches of the street beside the grace of those who exist in its netherworld, thanks to a homeless mentally ill woman.

The encounter forced me to contemplate that we all die—rich and poor alike. That knowledge should allow us to embrace our humility and our compassion, to seek guidance in whatever spiritual path comforts our life journey. It should also move us to acknowledge the fact that way too many mentally ill and physically sick people call our streets home. Regardless of our judgments about how they got there, they are here—and they are our neighbors. We should remember that we all possess a soul that transcends wealth and our stations in life. Judgment can be delivered not in this life but in the next. And that judgment will not be directed only at the homeless but at all of us, for how we treated those crippled by pain and broken by the human condition.

I know that sometimes I drive my wife crazy, because she is more outgoing than me. At times I find the casual chitchat of social affairs taxing. I'm more comfortable, more myself, on the streets talking to the mentally ill, arranging a medical visit by Dr. Jahnke, making a referral to Nurse Jan Fadden for those in need of medical services, or offering advice to those struggling with addiction. Party small talk comes hard to me: I know that it's part of who I am after working all these years on the streets. My wife is gracious and understanding. She has a generous soul, and I stand in awe of her beauty. She and my children are truly God's gift to me.

ABOUT THE AUTHOR

For over thirty years, Ken Williams has worked as a social worker for the homeless in Santa Barbara, California, for which he has won multiple awards. He is a Marine combat veteran of Vietnam, having served with the Ninth Marines—the Walking Dead. He writes extensively on the subjects of the war and homelessness for the local media. He is the author of *China White and Shattered Dreams, a Story of the Streets*. He currently resides in Santa Barbara with his wife, Donna.